HOUGHTON MIFFLIN HARC

Response to Intervention

FOR THE COMMON CORE STATE STANDARDS FOR MATHEMATICS

GRADE 2

**PROVIDES Tier 2 Skills and Tier 3 Examples
for Every Tier 1 Lesson**

Forest Road School
LaGrange Park, IL 60526

HOUGHTON MIFFLIN HARCOURT

Table of Contents

© Houghton Mifflin Harcourt Publishing Company

SKILL S1 **Same Number**

OBJECTIVE Identify sets that have the same number of objects.

You can match objects in two sets.

If each object has a match without any left over, then the two sets have the **same number** of objects.

Use ⬤ ⬤ two sets of objects that have the same number of objects. Draw to show your work.

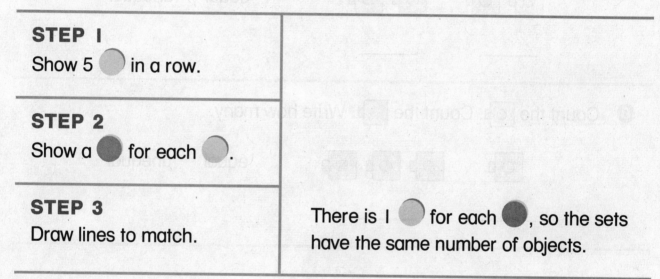

STEP 1
Show 5 ⬤ in a row.

STEP 2
Show a ⬤ for each ⬤.

STEP 3
Draw lines to match.

There is 1 ⬤ for each ⬤, so the sets have the same number of objects.

Try This!

Show that the sets have the same number of objects.

Draw a line to match each ⬤ to a ⬤.

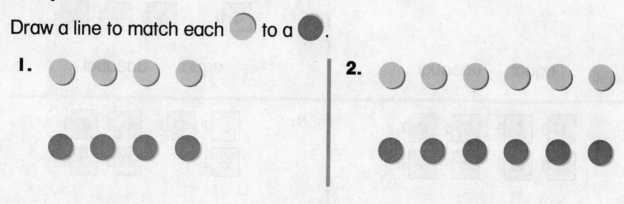

1.

2.

SKILL S2 — Equal and Unequal Groups

OBJECTIVE Determine if groups of objects are equal or unequal.

Equal groups show the same number of objects.
Unequal groups show different number of objects.

Count how many in each group.
Circle **equal** or **unequal**.

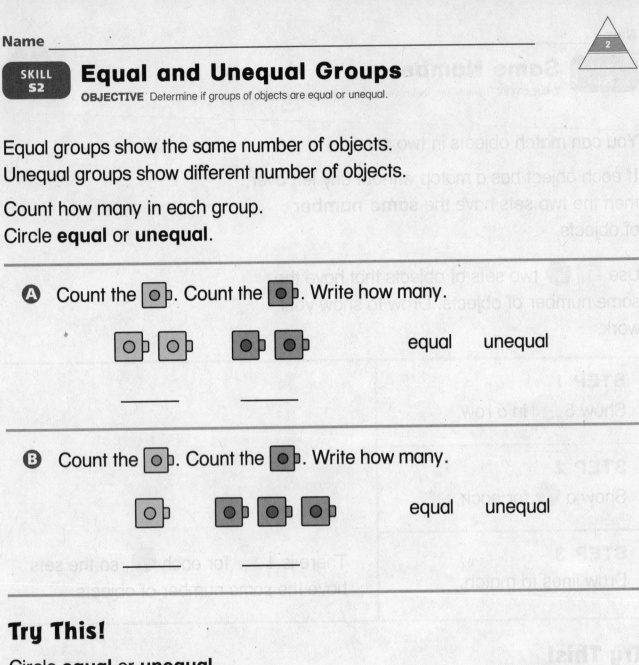

A Count the ▢. Count the ▢. Write how many.

equal   unequal

_____   _____

B Count the ▢. Count the ▢. Write how many.

equal   unequal

_____   _____

Try This!

Circle **equal** or **unequal**.

1.

equal   unequal

2.

equal   unequal

3.

equal   unequal

4.

equal   unequal

SKILL S3   Count and Write Numbers to 10

OBJECTIVE Use concrete objects to count and model numbers to 10.

You can use ☐ to count and show numbers.

Model and write the number 5.

STEP 1 Use 5 ☐ to show the number 5.	5
STEP 2 Draw the cubes.	
STEP 3 Write the number.	____

Try This!

Use ☐ to show each number.

Draw the ☐ .

Write the number.

1. 6	**2.** 8
____	____

SKILL S4 **First, Next, Last**

OBJECTIVE Read number patterns to write which numbers are first, next, and last.

A number pattern can help you tell which numbers are first, next, and last.

Look at the number pattern.
Tell what numbers are first, next, and last.

STEP 1 The first number begins the pattern. Write the first number.	8 9 10 eight, nine, ten
STEP 2 The next number comes after the first number. Write the next number.	**Think:** Each number is one more than the one before it.
STEP 3 The last number ends the pattern. Write the last number.	____ ____ ____ first next last

Try This!

Look at the number pattern.

        5   6   7

1. What number is first? _____   **2.** What number is next? _____

        12   13   14

3. What number is last? _____   **4.** What number is first? _____

SKILL S5 **Identify Numbers to 30**

OBJECTIVE Model numbers to 30 on ten frames.

You can use ⬤ to show a number.

Count to find how many.

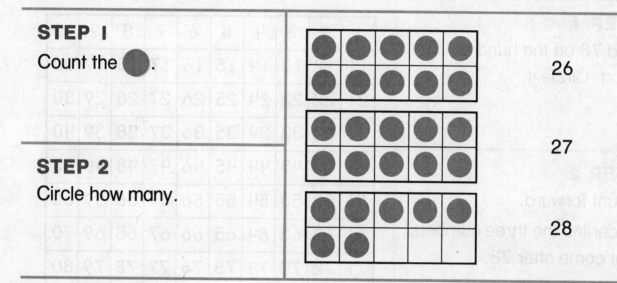

STEP 1

Count the ⬤.

26

STEP 2

Circle how many.

27

28

Try This!

Count the ⬤.
Circle how many.

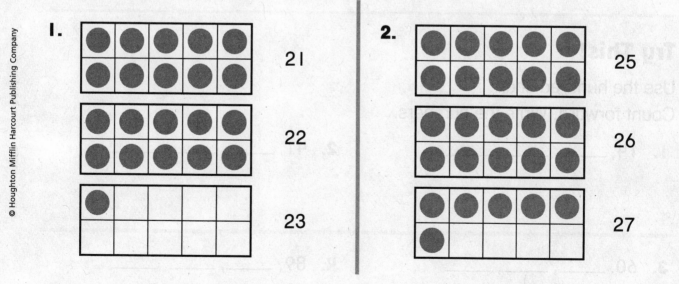

1.

21

22

23

2.

25

26

27

SKILL S6 Count by Ones to 100

OBJECTIVE Count by ones to extend a counting sequence to 100.

You can count by ones on a hundred chart.

Count forward from 78. Write the numbers.

STEP 1	
Find 78 on the hundred chart. Circle it.	

STEP 2

Count forward.

Underline the three numbers that come after 78.

STEP 3

Write the numbers.

1	2	3	4	5	6	7	8	9	10
11	12	13	14	15	16	17	18	19	20
21	22	23	24	25	26	27	28	29	30
31	32	33	34	35	36	37	38	39	40
41	42	43	44	45	46	47	48	49	50
51	52	53	54	55	56	57	58	59	60
61	62	63	64	65	66	67	68	69	70
71	72	73	74	75	76	77	78	79	80
81	82	83	84	85	86	87	88	89	90
91	92	93	94	95	96	97	98	99	100

78, _____, _____, _____

Try This!

Use the hundred chart.

Count forward. Write the numbers.

1. 14, _____, _____, _____

2. 41, _____, _____, _____

3. 60, _____, _____, _____

4. 89, _____, _____, _____

SKILL S7 **Count by Tens**

OBJECTIVE Use concrete objects to count by tens.

You can use 🔲 to count by tens.

Use groups of 10 🔲. Count by tens to 30.
Draw the 🔲. Write the numbers.

STEP 1 Show 10 🔲. Write how many 🔲.	
STEP 2 Show 10 🔲 more. Write how many 🔲 now.	
STEP 3 Show 10 🔲 more. Write the total number of 🔲.	_____, _____, _____

Try This!

Use 🔲. Count by tens.

1.

_____, _____

2.

_____, _____, _____, _____, _____

Name _____

SKILL S8 **Count by Twos, Fives, and Tens**

OBJECTIVE Use concrete objects to count by twos, fives, and tens.

You can count by twos, fives, and tens to count objects in a group.

Write the number.

A Count by twos.

2,   4,   6,   _____

B Count by fives.

5,   10,   _____

C Count by tens.

10,   20,   30,   _____

Try This!

Write the numbers.

1.

2,   4,   _____,   8,   _____

2.

5,   10,   _____

© Houghton Mifflin Harcourt Publishing Company

SKILL S9 · Make a Model · Names for Numbers

OBJECTIVE Compose numbers in different ways.

2

You can use [■] and [□] to show numbers in different ways.

Show two ways to make 8. Color the cubes to match.

Ⓐ Use 1 [■] and 7 [□].

Complete the addition sentence.

[○ ○ ○ ○ ○ ○ ○ ○]

_____ [■] + _____ [□] = _____

Ⓑ Use 2 [■] and 6 [□].

Complete the addition sentence.

[○ ○ ○ ○ ○ ○ ○ ○]

_____ [■] + _____ [□] = _____

Try This!

Use [■] and [□]. Show two ways to make 7.
Color the cubes to match. Complete the addition
sentences.

1.   [○ ○ ○ ○ ○ ○ ○]

_____ [■] + _____ [□] = _____

2.   [○ ○ ○ ○ ○ ○ ○]

_____ [■] + _____ [□] = _____

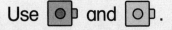

SKILL S10

Use Symbols to Add

OBJECTIVE Use the symbols + and = to find sums.

You can use + and = to add.

Add 2 and 3.

Use and .

Draw to show your work.

STEP 1

Show 2 .

STEP 2

Show 3 .

STEP 3

Complete the addition sentence.

Write how many in all.

Think: 2 plus 3 equals _____

2 + 3 = _____

Try This!

Complete the addition sentence.

Write how many in all.

1.

4 + 2 = _____

2.

1 + 1 = _____

SKILL S11 — Algebra • Use Drawings to Represent Add to and Put Together Problems

OBJECTIVE Model and draw to solve "add to" and "put together" addition problems.

You can use 🔲 and a bar model to find the sum.

There are 4 black bears. 3 brown bears join them.
How many bears are there now?

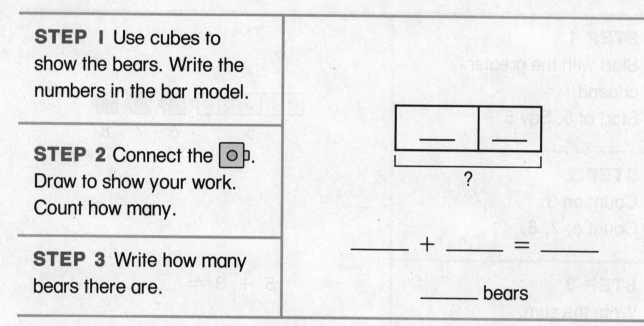

STEP 1 Use cubes to show the bears. Write the numbers in the bar model.
STEP 2 Connect the 🔲. Draw to show your work. Count how many.
STEP 3 Write how many bears there are.

_____ + _____ = _____

_____ bears

Try This!

Use 🔲 and a bar model. Draw to show your work.
Complete the addition sentence.

1. Mark has 2 stickers. Then he gets 4 more stickers. How many stickers does Mark have now?

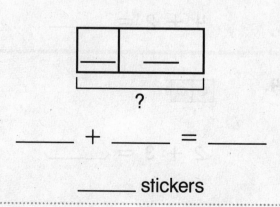

_____ + _____ = _____

_____ stickers

2. There are 3 blue birds on a branch. 2 red birds join them. How many birds are there now?

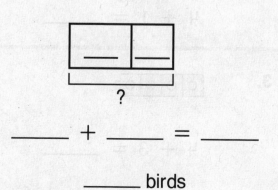

_____ + _____ = _____

_____ birds

SKILL S12 # Count On to Add

OBJECTIVE Count on 1, 2, and 3 from numbers to 9.

You can count on 1, 2, and 3 to add.

Count on. Write the sum.

STEP 1 Start with the greater addend. Start at 5. Say 5.	5 6 7 8
STEP 2 Count on 3. Count 6, 7, 8.	
STEP 3 Write the sum.	5 + 3 = _____

Try This!

Draw the cubes to count on. Write the sum.

1.

4 + 1 = _____

2.

4 + 2 = _____

3.

4 + 3 = _____

4.

2 + 3 = _____

SKILL S13 Algebra • Add in Any Order

OBJECTIVE Use concrete objects to explore the Order Property of Addition.

You can add the same numbers in any order and get the same sum.

Use 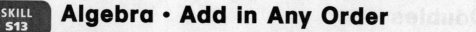 and ⬤ to add.
Draw two ways to get the same sum.

STEP 1 Add 2 + 3. Write the sum.	$2 + 3 = $ _____
STEP 2 Add 3 + 2. Write the sum.	$3 + 2 = $ _____

Try This!

Use ⬜ and ⬤ to add. Write each sum.
Color to match.

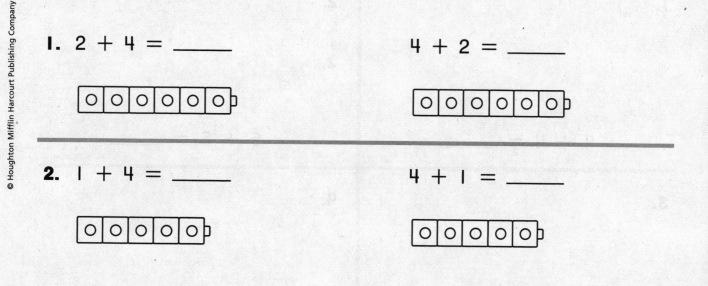

1. $2 + 4 = $ _____ $4 + 2 = $ _____

2. $1 + 4 = $ _____ $4 + 1 = $ _____

SKILL S14 **Add Doubles**

OBJECTIVE Use doubles as a strategy to solve addition facts with sums within 20.

The addends are the same in a doubles fact.

Use 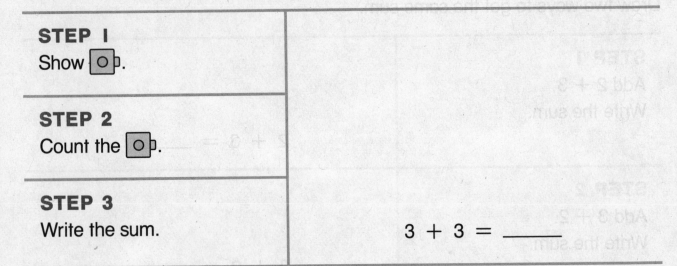 to show the addends. Count the ☐.

Write the sum. Draw to show your work.

STEP 1 Show ☐.	
STEP 2 Count the ☐.	
STEP 3 Write the sum.	3 + 3 = _____

Try This!

Use ☐. Count the ☐. Write the sum.

Draw to show your work.

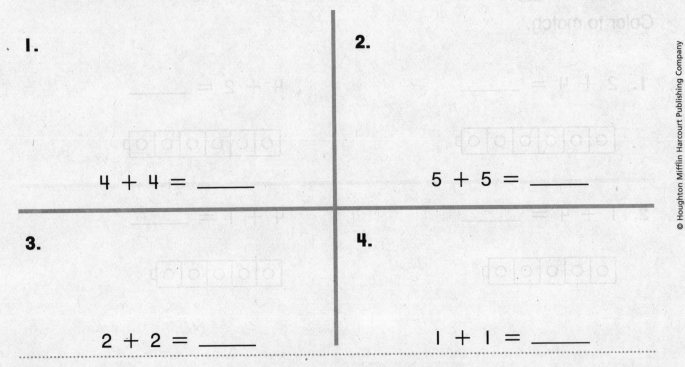

1.

4 + 4 = _____

2.

5 + 5 = _____

3.

2 + 2 = _____

4.

1 + 1 = _____

SKILL S15 Doubles and Doubles Plus One

OBJECTIVE Use doubles and doubles plus one as strategies to find sums.

You can use doubles and doubles plus one facts
to find the sum.

Use . Use doubles and double plus one facts.
Write the sums.

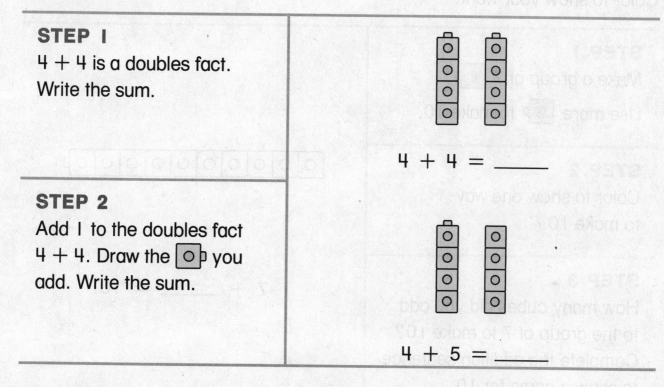

STEP 1	
4 + 4 is a doubles fact. Write the sum.	$4 + 4 = \underline{\hspace{1cm}}$
STEP 2	
Add 1 to the doubles fact 4 + 4. Draw the ☐ you add. Write the sum.	$4 + 5 = \underline{\hspace{1cm}}$

Try This!

Use ☐. Write the addition sentence.

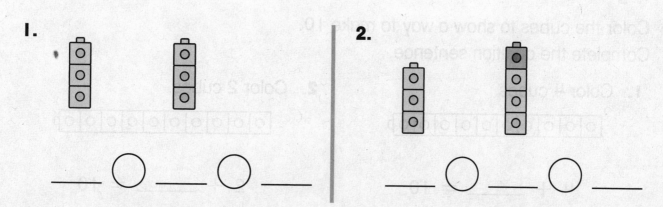

1.

$\underline{\hspace{1cm}} \bigcirc \underline{\hspace{1cm}} \bigcirc \underline{\hspace{1cm}}$

2.

$\underline{\hspace{1cm}} \bigcirc \underline{\hspace{1cm}} \bigcirc \underline{\hspace{1cm}}$

SKILL S16

Identify Names for 10

OBJECTIVE Use concrete objects to find different names for 10.

You can group and ▢ in different ways to make 10.

Use cubes of two colors to show a way to make 10.

Color to show your work.

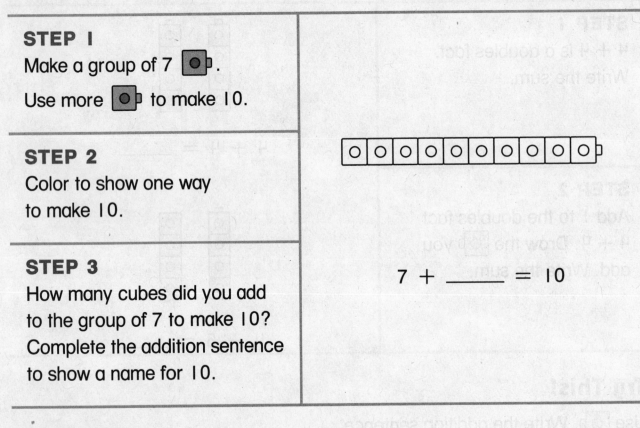

STEP 1

Make a group of 7 ▢.

Use more ▢ to make 10.

STEP 2

Color to show one way to make 10.

STEP 3

How many cubes did you add to the group of 7 to make 10? Complete the addition sentence to show a name for 10.

$$7 + \rule{1.5cm}{0.4pt} = 10$$

Try This!

Color the cubes to show a way to make 10.

Complete the addition sentence.

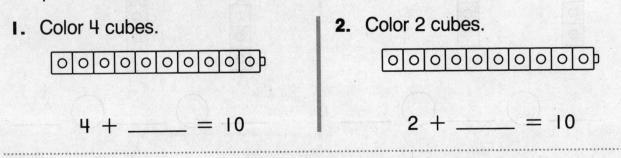

1. Color 4 cubes.

$$4 + \rule{1.5cm}{0.4pt} = 10$$

2. Color 2 cubes.

$$2 + \rule{1.5cm}{0.4pt} = 10$$

SKILL S17 · Make a Ten

OBJECTIVE Model the strategy make a ten to find sums to 18.

You can make a ten to help find the sum
for numbers greater than 10.

Use a ten frame and ⬤ to find the sum
of 7 + 5. Start with the greater number.

STEP 1 Put 7 counters in the ten frame. Put 5 counters outside.	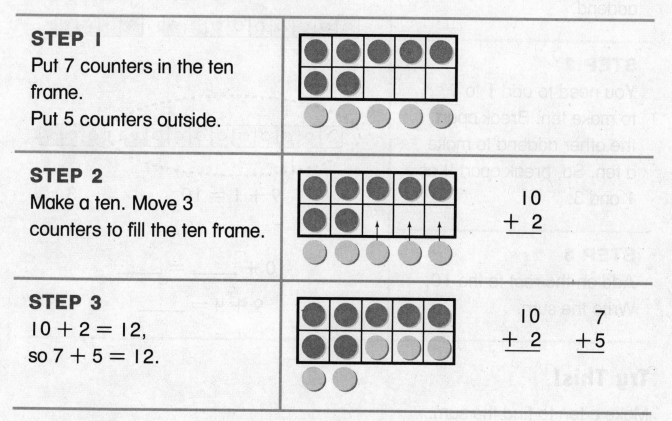
STEP 2 Make a ten. Move 3 counters to fill the ten frame.	$\begin{array}{r} 10 \\ +\ 2 \\ \hline \end{array}$
STEP 3 10 + 2 = 12, so 7 + 5 = 12.	$\begin{array}{r} 10 \\ +\ 2 \\ \hline \end{array}$ $\begin{array}{r} 7 \\ +5 \\ \hline \end{array}$

Try This!

Use a ten frame and ⬤ to make a ten.
Find the sum.

1. $\begin{array}{r} 9 \\ +5 \\ \hline \end{array}$	2. $\begin{array}{r} 6 \\ +7 \\ \hline \end{array}$	3. $\begin{array}{r} 4 \\ +8 \\ \hline \end{array}$	4. $\begin{array}{r} 8 \\ +8 \\ \hline \end{array}$

SKILL S18 Algebra • Make a Ten to Add

OBJECTIVE Use the make a ten strategy to add.

Use make a ten to help you add.

Find the sum of 9 + 4.

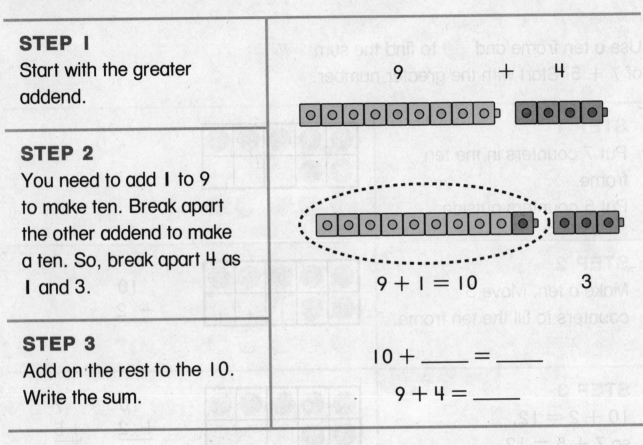

STEP 1 Start with the greater addend.	9 + 4
STEP 2 You need to add 1 to 9 to make ten. Break apart the other addend to make a ten. So, break apart 4 as 1 and 3.	9 + 1 = 10 3
STEP 3 Add on the rest to the 10. Write the sum.	10 + ____ = ____ 9 + 4 = ____

Try This!

Make a ten to find the sum.
Write the sum.

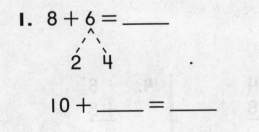

1. 8 + 6 = ____

    2 4

    10 + ____ = ____

2. 7 + 9 = ____

    3 6

    10 + ____ = ____

© Houghton Mifflin Harcourt Publishing Company

SKILL S19 Addition Patterns

OBJECTIVE Act out adding 1 to a group.

When you count forward, you add 1.

Add 3 + 1.

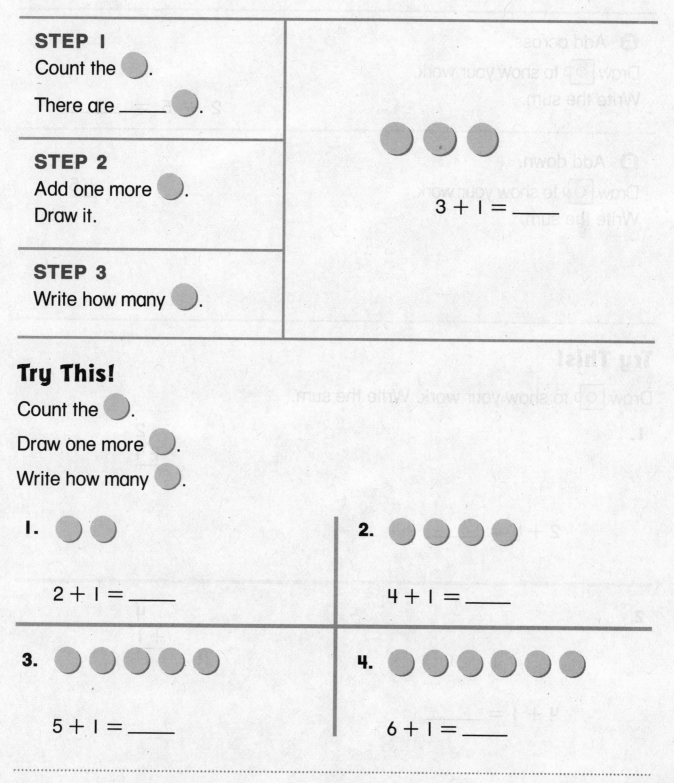

STEP 1
Count the ⬤.
There are _____ ⬤.

STEP 2
Add one more ⬤.
Draw it.

STEP 3
Write how many ⬤.

3 + 1 = _____

Try This!

Count the ⬤.
Draw one more ⬤.
Write how many ⬤.

1. ⬤⬤

2 + 1 = _____

2. ⬤⬤⬤⬤

4 + 1 = _____

3. ⬤⬤⬤⬤⬤

5 + 1 = _____

4. ⬤⬤⬤⬤⬤⬤

6 + 1 = _____

SKILL S20 · Sums to 10

OBJECTIVE Demonstrate fluency for addition with sums to 10.

You can add down or across.
The sum is the same.

Ⓐ Add across.
Draw ⬜ to show your work.
Write the sum.

$2 + 5 = $ _____

Ⓑ Add down.
Draw ⬜ to show your work.
Write the sum.

$$\begin{array}{r} 2 \\ +5 \\ \hline \end{array}$$

Try This!

Draw ⬜ to show your work. Write the sum.

1.

$$\begin{array}{r} 2 \\ +4 \\ \hline \end{array}$$

$2 + 4 = $ _____

2.

$$\begin{array}{r} 4 \\ +1 \\ \hline \end{array}$$

$4 + 1 = $ _____

SKILL S21

Sums to 12

OBJECTIVE Use concrete objects to find sums to 12.

There are many ways to find a sum.

Use 5  and 7 🔲 to add 5 and 7.

STEP 1
Draw to show your work.

STEP 2
Write how many 🔲 and how many 🔲.

STEP 3
Complete the addition sentence. Add. Write the sum.

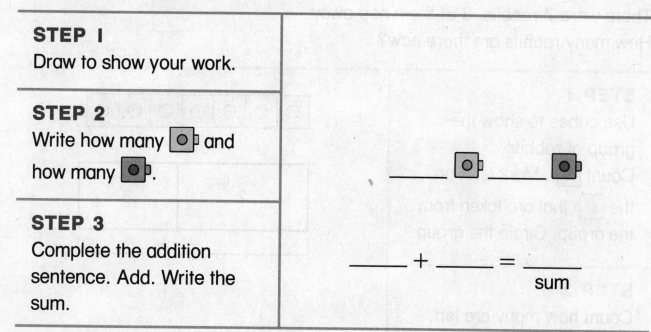

____ ____

____ + ____ = _____
            sum

Try This!

Complete the addition sentence.
Add. Write the sum.

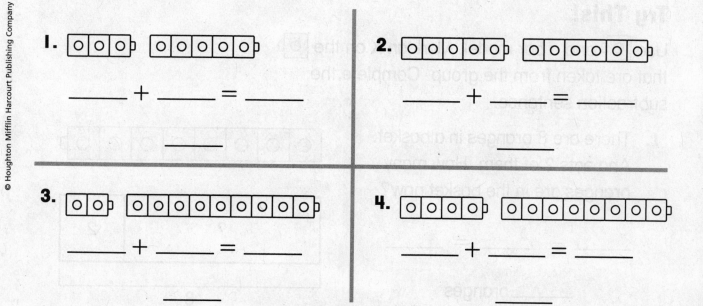

1. ____ + ____ = ____

____

2. ____ + ____ = ____

____

3. ____ + ____ = ____

____

4. ____ + ____ = ____

____

SKILL S22

Algebra • Use Drawings to Represent Take From or Take Apart Problems

OBJECTIVE Use connecting cubes and bar models to solve "take apart" subtraction problems.

You can use 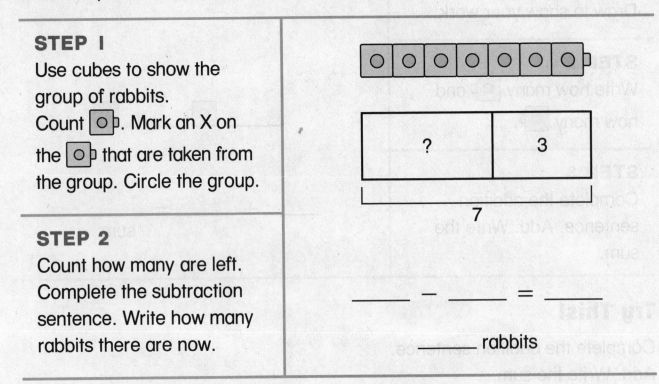 and a bar model to find the difference.

There were 7 rabbits. 3 of them hop away.
How many rabbits are there now?

STEP 1

Use cubes to show the group of rabbits.
Count ☐. Mark an X on the ☐ that are taken from the group. Circle the group.

STEP 2

Count how many are left. Complete the subtraction sentence. Write how many rabbits there are now.

? | 3

7

_____ – _____ = _____

_____ rabbits

Try This!

Use ☐ and a bar model. Mark an X on the ☐ that are taken from the group. Complete the subtraction sentence.

1. There are 8 oranges in a basket. Ana eats 2 of them. How many oranges are in the basket now?

_____ – _____ = _____

_____ oranges

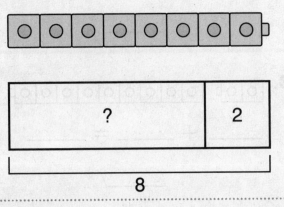

? | 2

8

Name _____

SKILL S23 **Algebra · Use Drawings to Represent Compare Problems**

OBJECTIVE Model and compare groups to show the meaning of subtraction.

You can use 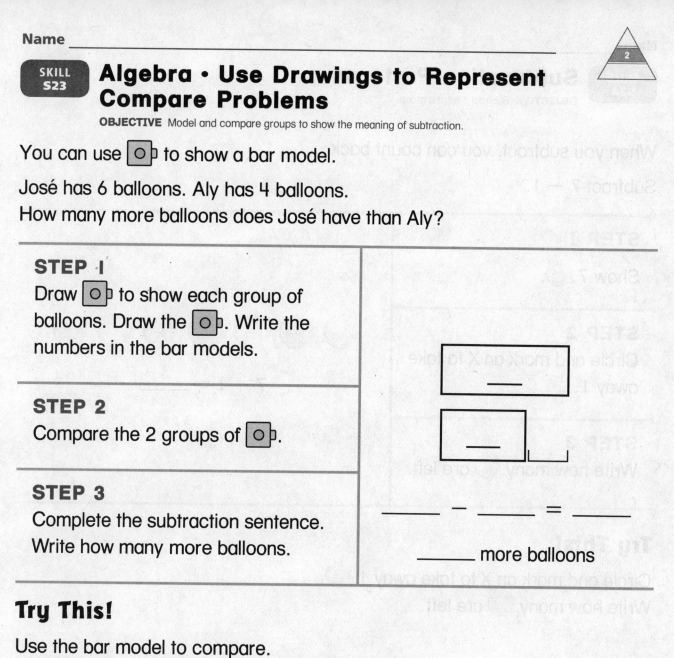 to show a bar model.

José has 6 balloons. Aly has 4 balloons.
How many more balloons does José have than Aly?

STEP 1
Draw ▣ to show each group of balloons. Draw the ▣. Write the numbers in the bar models.

STEP 2
Compare the 2 groups of ▣.

STEP 3
Complete the subtraction sentence. Write how many more balloons.

_____ – _____ = _____

_____ more balloons

Try This!

Use the bar model to compare.

Draw the ▣ to show each group.

1. Ann has 9 pens. Tim has 5 pens. How many fewer pens does Tim have than Ann?

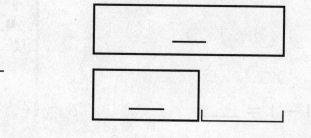

_____ – _____ = _____

_____ fewer pens

© Houghton Mifflin Harcourt Publishing Company

Subtraction Patterns

OBJECTIVE Subtract 1 from a group.

When you subtract, you can count back.

Subtract 7 − 1.

STEP 1

Show 7 .

STEP 2

Circle and mark an X to take away 1.

STEP 3

Write how many ◯ are left.

7 − 1 = ____

Try This!

Circle and mark an X to take away 1 ◯.

Write how many ◯ are left.

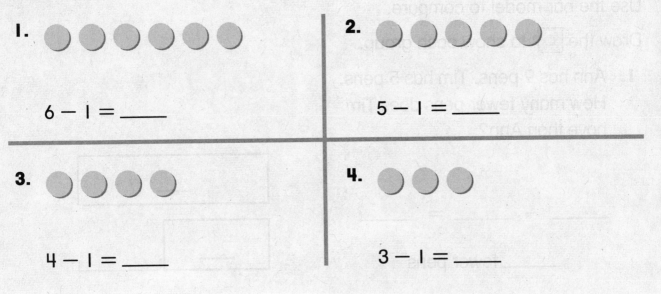

1. 6 − 1 = ____

2. 5 − 1 = ____

3. 4 − 1 = ____

4. 3 − 1 = ____

SKILL S25 Differences to 10

OBJECTIVE Demonstrate fluency for subtraction with differences to 10.

You can subtract down or across.
The difference is the same.

A Subtract across.
Draw to show your work.
Write the difference.

$$7 - 5 = \rule{2cm}{0.4pt}$$

B Subtract down.
Draw to show your work.
Write the difference.

$$\begin{array}{r} 7 \\ -5 \\ \hline \end{array}$$

Try This!

Draw to show your work.
Write the difference.

1.

$$\begin{array}{r} 6 \\ -3 \\ \hline \end{array}$$

$$6 - 3 = \rule{2cm}{0.4pt}$$

2.

$$\begin{array}{r} 5 \\ -1 \\ \hline \end{array}$$

$$5 - 1 = \rule{2cm}{0.4pt}$$

SKILL S26 · **Algebra · Relate Addition and Subtraction**

OBJECTIVE Use concrete objects to relate addition and subtraction.

Knowing a related addition fact can help you subtract.

Use ⬜ to find the sum or difference.

Draw to show your work.

STEP 1 Start with 3 and count on 2. Find the sum.	$3 + 2 =$ _____
STEP 2 Use a related fact to subtract. Start with 5 and count back 2. Find the difference. **Think:** $2 + 3 = 5$	$5 - 2 =$ _____

Try This!

Use ⬜. Write the sum or difference.

Draw to show your work.

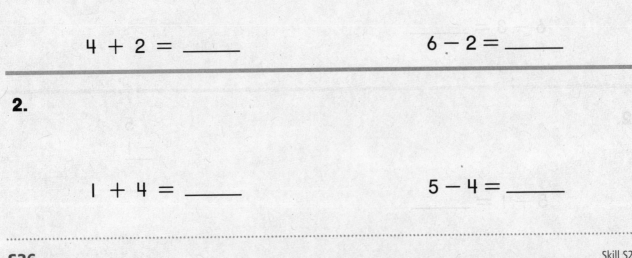

1.

$4 + 2 =$ _____ $\qquad$ $6 - 2 =$ _____

2.

$1 + 4 =$ _____ $\qquad$ $5 - 4 =$ _____

2

SKILL S27 **Count Back**

OBJECTIVE Count back to subtract.

You can **count back** 1, 2, or 3 to subtract.

Use 7 ⚫. Count back 2.

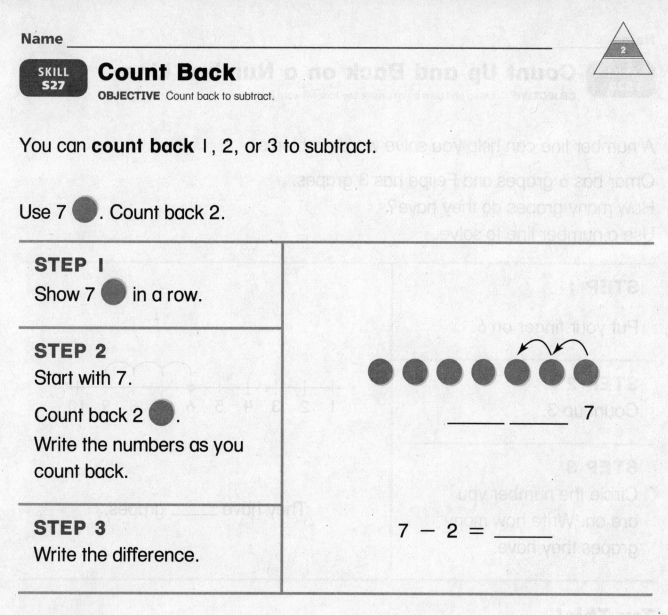

STEP 1
Show 7 ⚫ in a row.

STEP 2
Start with 7.

Count back 2 ⚫.
Write the numbers as you
count back.

STEP 3
Write the difference.

_____ _____ 7

$7 - 2 = $ _____

Try This!

Use ⚫. Count back 1, 2, or 3.

Write the numbers as you count back.

Write the difference.

1.

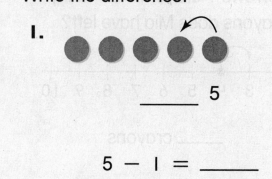

_____ 5

$5 - 1 = $ _____

2.

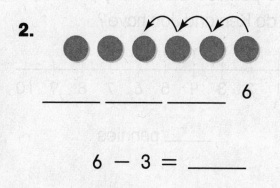

_____ _____ _____ 6

$6 - 3 = $ _____

Count Up and Back on a Number Line

OBJECTIVE Count up and back on a number line to solve word problems.

A number line can help you solve word problems.

Omar has 6 grapes and Felipe has 3 grapes.
How many grapes do they have?
Use a number line to solve.

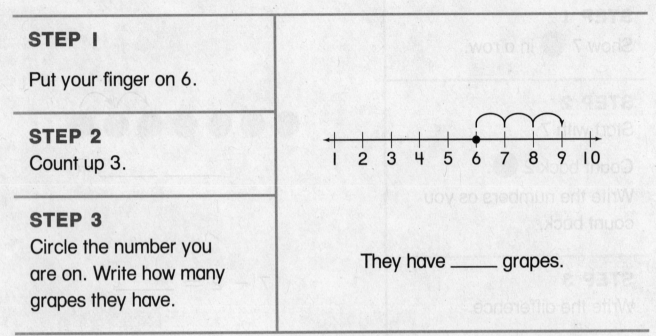

STEP 1

Put your finger on 6.

STEP 2

Count up 3.

STEP 3

Circle the number you are on. Write how many grapes they have.

They have _____ grapes.

Try This!

Use the number line to solve the word problem.

1. Ken has 2 pennies. Jon has 3 pennies. How many pennies do Ken and Jon have?

   _____ pennies

2. Mia has 4 crayons. Liam borrows 1 crayon. How many crayons does Mia have left?

   _____ crayons

SKILL S29 — Use Ten to Subtract

OBJECTIVE Decompose a ten to help find differences.

You can get to ten to help find differences.

Find the difference of $12 - 7$.

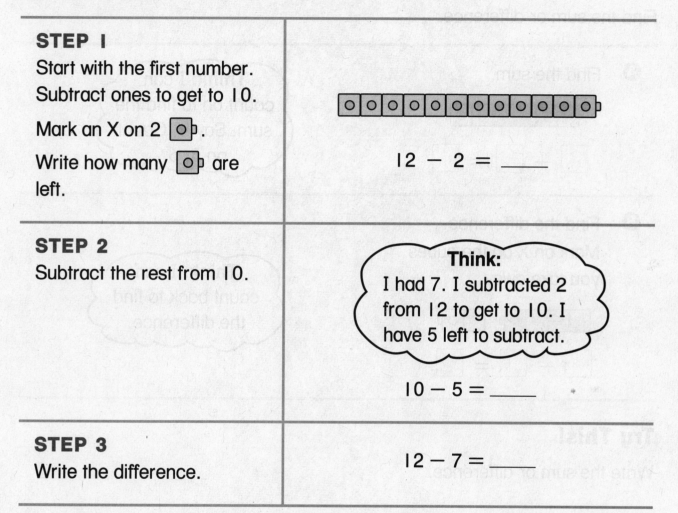

STEP 1

Start with the first number.
Subtract ones to get to 10.

Mark an X on 2 .

Write how many are left.

$12 - 2 = $ _____

STEP 2

Subtract the rest from 10.

Think:
I had 7. I subtracted 2 from 12 to get to 10. I have 5 left to subtract.

$10 - 5 = $ _____

STEP 3

Write the difference.

$12 - 7 = $ _____

Try This!

Use the tens facts. Write the difference.

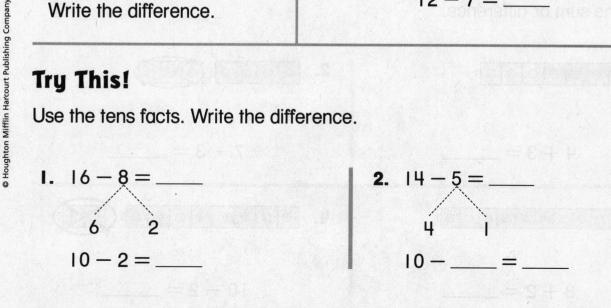

1. $16 - 8 = $ _____

6   2

$10 - 2 = $ _____

2. $14 - 5 = $ _____

4   1

$10 - $ _____ $ = $ _____

SKILL S30

Sums and Differences to 10

OBJECTIVE Count on to add and count back to subtract.

You can count on to add and count back to subtract.

Find the sum or difference.

A Find the sum.

☐ + ☐ = ☐

> **Think:** I can count on to find the sum. Say 4. Count on 5, 6.

B Find the difference.
Mark an X on the cubes you take away.

☐ − ☐ = ☐

> **Think:** I can count back to find the difference.

Try This!

Write the sum or difference.

I.

$4 + 3 =$ _____

2.

$7 - 3 =$ _____

3.

$8 + 2 =$ _____

4.

$10 - 2 =$ _____

2

SKILL S31

Explore Tens

OBJECTIVE Identify groups that show 10; count by tens.

When you count many objects, make groups of ten.

Use 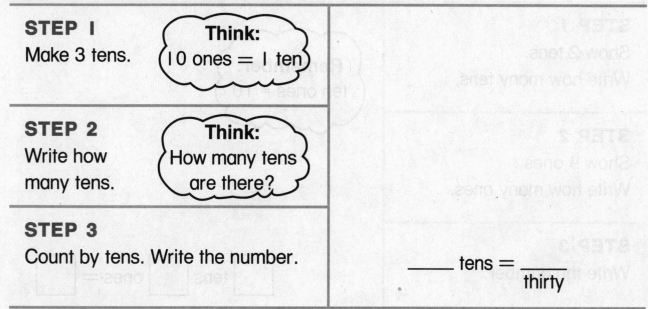 to make 3 tens. Write the number.
Draw to show your work.

STEP 1
Make 3 tens.

Think:
10 ones = 1 ten

STEP 2
Write how
many tens.

Think:
How many tens
are there?

STEP 3
Count by tens. Write the number.

_____ tens = _____
          thirty

Try This!

Use 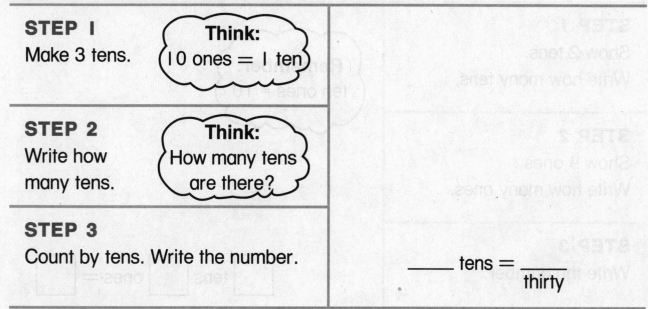 to make tens.
Count by tens. Write the number.

1.

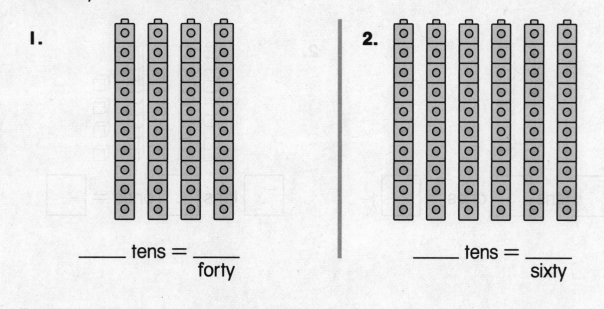

_____ tens = _____
          forty

2.

_____ tens = _____
          sixty

SKILL S32

Explore Tens and Ones to 100

OBJECTIVE Use concrete objectes to identify tens and ones.

You can use 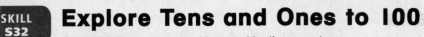 to show numbers.

Use ▭ to show 2 tens 4 ones.
Draw to show your work. Write the number.

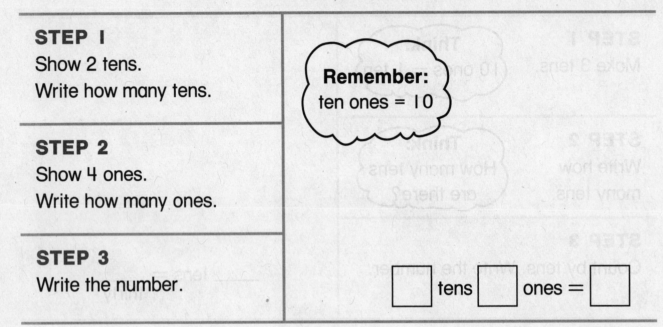

STEP 1

Show 2 tens.
Write how many tens.

STEP 2

Show 4 ones.
Write how many ones.

STEP 3

Write the number.

Remember:
ten ones = 10

☐ tens ☐ ones = ☐

Try This!

Use ▭ ☐. Write how many tens and ones. Write the number.

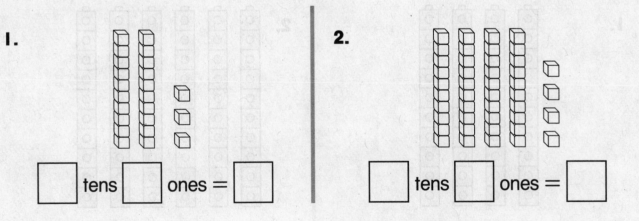

I. ☐ tens ☐ ones = ☐

2. ☐ tens ☐ ones = ☐

© Houghton Mifflin Harcourt Publishing Company

SKILL S33
Model Tens and Ones to 100

OBJECTIVE Group objects to show numbers to 100 as tens and ones.

If you know the tens and the ones, you can write the number.

Use ▭▭▭ ▯ to show 5 tens 7 ones.
Draw to show your work. Write the number.

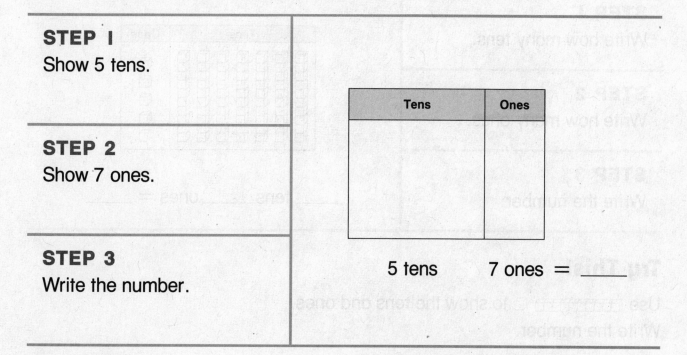

STEP 1 Show 5 tens.	
STEP 2 Show 7 ones.	
STEP 3 Write the number.	

Tens	Ones

5 tens   7 ones = _____

Try This!

Use ▭▭▭ ▯ to show the tens and ones.
Draw to show your work.
Write the number.

1. 4 tens 5 ones = _____

2. 6 tens 3 ones = _____

SKILL S34 Tens and Ones to 100

OBJECTIVE Model and write numbers to 100.

You can use ▭▭▭▭ ▫ to show numbers to 100.

Use ▭▭▭▭ ▫ to show the tens and ones.
Write the number.

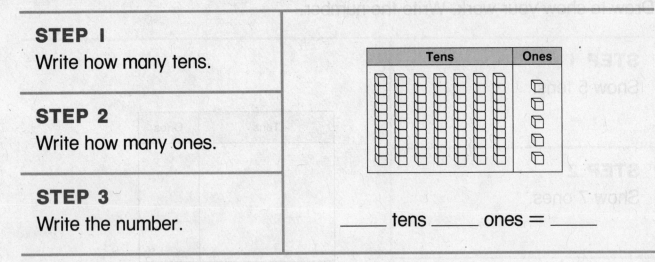

STEP 1	
Write how many tens.	
STEP 2	
Write how many ones.	
STEP 3	
Write the number.	

_____ tens _____ ones = _____

Try This!

Use ▭▭▭▭ ▫ to show the tens and ones.
Write the number.

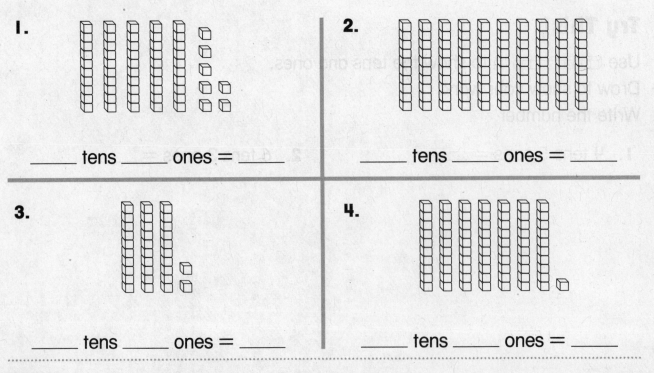

1.

_____ tens _____ ones = _____

2.

_____ tens _____ ones = _____

3.

_____ tens _____ ones = _____

4.

_____ tens _____ ones = _____

SKILL S35 — Understand Place Value

OBJECTIVE Use concrete objects to understand place value in 2-digit numbers.

0, 1, 2, 3, 4, 5, 6, 7, 8, and 9 are digits.
The place that a digit is in tells you how much
the digit stands for. This is its value.

Find the value of each digit in 35
Draw to show your work.

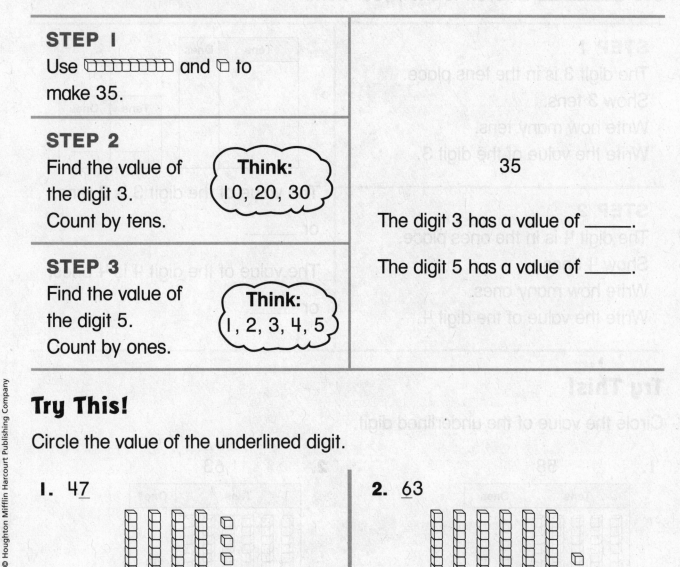

STEP 1
Use ▭ and ▫ to
make 35.

STEP 2
Find the value of
the digit 3.
Count by tens.

Think:
10, 20, 30

STEP 3
Find the value of
the digit 5.
Count by ones.

Think:
1, 2, 3, 4, 5

35

The digit 3 has a value of _____.

The digit 5 has a value of _____.

Try This!

Circle the value of the underlined digit.

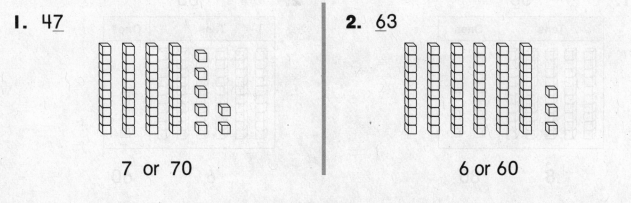

1. 4<u>7</u>

7 or 70

2. <u>6</u>3

6 or 60

SKILL S36

Place Value: 2-Digit Numbers

OBJECTIVE Understand that the digits of a 2-digit number represent tens and ones.

0, 1, 2, 3, 4, 5, 6, 7, 8, and 9 are digits.

In a 2-digit number, you know the value

of a digit by its place value.

What is the value of each digit in 34?

Use 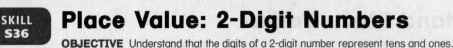. Draw to show your work.

STEP 1

The digit 3 is in the tens place.

Show 3 tens.

Write how many tens.

Write the value of the digit 3.

STEP 2

The digit 4 is in the ones place.

Show 4 ones.

Write how many ones.

Write the value of the digit 4.

Tens	Ones

Tens	Ones
___	___

The value of the digit 3 is 3 tens,

or _____.

The value of the digit 4 is 4 ones,

or _____.

Try This!

Circle the value of the underlined digit.

1.   5<u>8</u>

Tens	Ones

8   80

2.   <u>6</u>3

Tens	Ones

6   60

SKILL S37 **Different Ways to Write Numbers**

OBJECTIVE Write 2-digit numbers in word form, in expanded form, in standard form, and as tens and ones.

You can write numbers in different ways.

Show different ways to write the number 34.

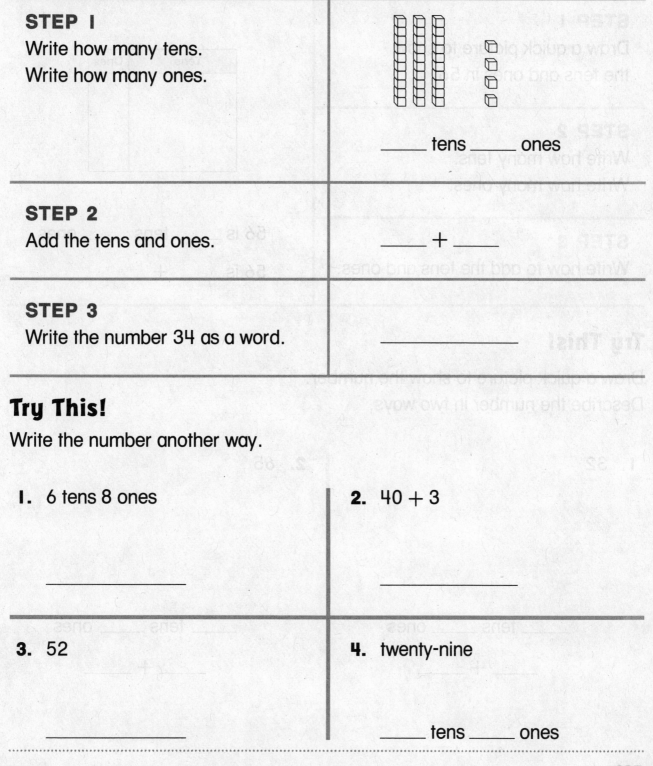

STEP 1

Write how many tens.
Write how many ones.

_____ tens _____ ones

STEP 2

Add the tens and ones.

_____ + _____

STEP 3

Write the number 34 as a word.

_____

Try This!

Write the number another way.

1. 6 tens 8 ones

_____

2. 40 + 3

_____

3. 52

_____

4. twenty-nine

_____ tens _____ ones

SKILL S38

Expanded Form

OBJECTIVE Write 2-digit numbers as tens and ones and in expanded form.

You can describe 2-digit numbers using tens and ones.

Use tens and ones to describe the number 56.

STEP 1

Draw a quick picture to show
the tens and ones in 56.

STEP 2

Write how many tens.
Write how many ones.

Tens	Ones

STEP 3

Write how to add the tens and ones.

56 is _____ tens _____ ones

56 is _____ + _____

Try This!

Draw a quick picture to show the number.
Describe the number in two ways.

1. 32

_____ tens _____ ones

_____ + _____

2. 65

_____ tens _____ ones

_____ + _____

SKILL S39

10 Less, 10 More

OBJECTIVE Identify numbers that are 10 less or 10 more than a given number.

You can use mental math to find numbers that are 10 more or 10 less than a given number.

Write the numbers that are 10 less and 10 more than 32.
Use ▭▭ ▭. Draw to show your work.

STEP 1	**STEP 2**	**STEP 3**
Show the number 32.	Take away a ten to show 10 less. Write the number.	Add a ten to show 10 more. Write the number.
32	_____ is 10 less than 32.	_____ is 10 more than 32.

Try This!

Write the numbers that are 10 less and 10 more.

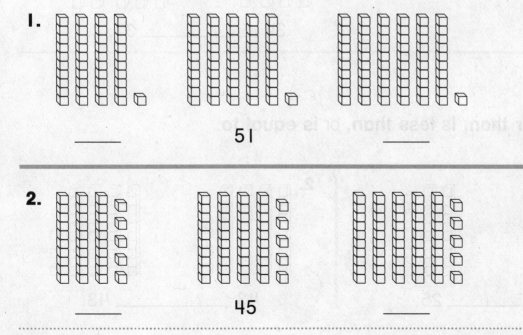

1. _____   51   _____

2. _____   45   _____

SKILL S40

Compare 2-Digit Numbers

OBJECTIVE Use is greater than, is less than, or is equal to to compare numbers.

You can use place value to compare numbers.

Compare 34 and 37.

STEP 1 Circle the tens. Compare the tens. Are the tens the same? _____ 3 tens is equal to 3 tens.	34 37
STEP 2 Circle the ones. Compare the ones. Are the ones the same? _____ 4 ones is less than 7 ones.	34 37
STEP 3 Write **is greater than, is less than,** or **is equal to.**	34 _____ 37.

Try This!

Write **is greater than, is less than,** or **is equal to.**

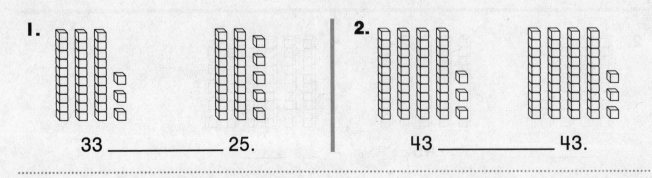

1.

33 _____ 25.

2.

43 _____ 43.

SKILL S41

Compare Numbers

OBJECTIVE Use >, =, and < to compare numbers.

You can use >, =, and < to compare numbers.

Compare 36 and 31.

STEP 1	
Circle the tens. Compare the tens. Are the tens the same? _____ 3 tens is equal to 3 tens.	36 31
STEP 2	
Circle the tens. Compare the ones. Are the ones the same? _____ 6 ones is greater than 1 one.	36 31
STEP 3	
Write <, =, or >.	36 ◯ 31

Try This!

Compare the numbers. Write <, =, or >.

1.   53 ◯ 54

2.   15 ◯ 15

SKILL S42 **Add Tens and Ones**

OBJECTIVE Use strategies based on place value to add 2-digit numbers without regrouping.

When you add two-digit numbers, add ones to ones and tens to tens.

Find 31 + 23.

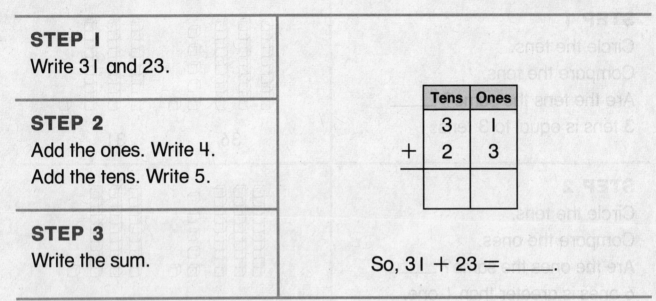

STEP 1

Write 31 and 23.

STEP 2

Add the ones. Write 4.
Add the tens. Write 5.

STEP 3

Write the sum.

Tens	Ones
3	1
+ 2	3

So, 31 + 23 = _____.

Try This!

Add.

1.

Tens	Ones
2	5
+ 3	4

2.

Tens	Ones
4	6
+ 2	0

3.

Tens	Ones
3	7
+ 3	1

4.

Tens	Ones
6	4
+ 1	3

Add On Tens

SKILL S43

OBJECTIVE Add multiples of ten.

You can use  to help you add on tens.

Find 36 + 20.

Use ⬚⬚⬚⬚⬚⬚ ▫. Draw to show your work.

STEP 1 Show 36. Then show 20.	
STEP 2 Say 36. Count on by tens. Write the numbers.	36, _____, _____
STEP 3 Write the sum.	So, 36 + 20 = _____

Try This!

Add on tens. Write the sum.

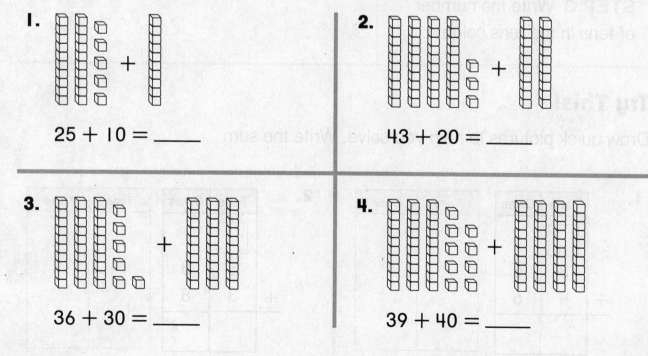

1. 25 + 10 = _____

2. 43 + 20 = _____

3. 36 + 30 = _____

4. 39 + 40 = _____

SKILL S44

Model and Record 2-Digit Addition

OBJECTIVE Model and record 2-digit addition using the standard algorithm.

You can model addends and help add.

Find the sum of 47 + 25.

STEP 1 Draw quick pictures to show 47 and 25. How many ones are there?

_____ ones

STEP 2 Regroup 10 ones as 1 ten. Write a 1 in the tens column to show the regrouped ten. Write a 2 in the ones column to show the ones that are left after regrouping.

STEP 3 Write the number of tens in the tens column.

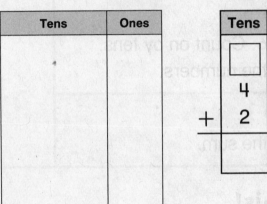

Tens	Ones

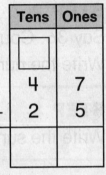

Tens	Ones
4	7
+ 2	5

Try This!

Draw quick pictures to help you solve. Write the sum.

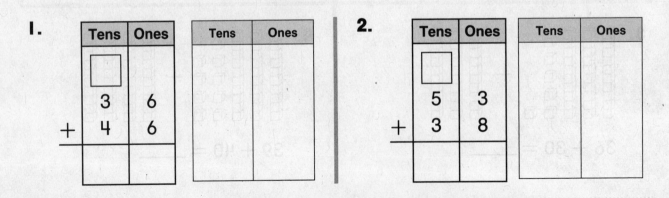

1.

Tens	Ones
3	6
+ 4	6

Tens	Ones

2.

Tens	Ones
5	3
+ 3	8

Tens	Ones

SKILL S45

Practice 2-Digit Addition

OBJECTIVE Practice 2-digit addition with and without regrouping.

When you add 2-digit numbers, you may need to regroup.

Add 43 + 39.

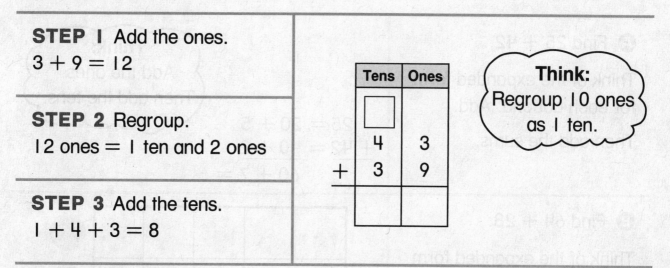

STEP 1 Add the ones.
3 + 9 = 12

STEP 2 Regroup.
12 ones = 1 ten and 2 ones

STEP 3 Add the tens.
1 + 4 + 3 = 8

Tens	Ones
4	3
+ 3	9

Think:
Regroup 10 ones as 1 ten.

Try This!

Write the sum. Regroup if you need to.

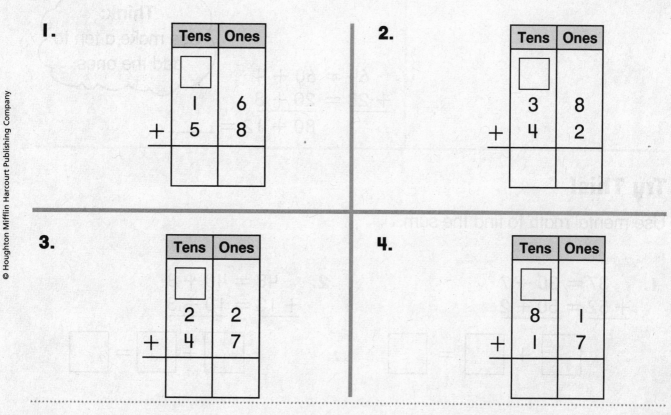

1.

Tens	Ones
1	6
+ 5	8

2.

Tens	Ones
3	8
+ 4	2

3.

Tens	Ones
2	2
+ 4	7

4.

Tens	Ones
8	1
+ 1	7

SKILL S46

Mental Math: Adding 2-Digit Numbers

OBJECTIVE Use mental math to add 2-digit numbers.

You can use mental math to add 2-digit numbers.

Use mental math to find the sums.

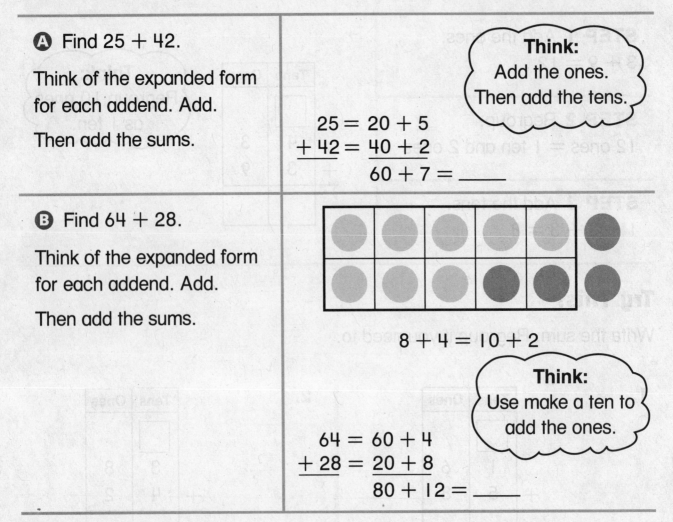

Ⓐ Find $25 + 42$.

Think of the expanded form for each addend. Add.

Then add the sums.

Think:
Add the ones.
Then add the tens.

$$25 = 20 + 5$$
$$+\ 42 = 40 + 2$$
$$60 + 7 = \underline{}$$

Ⓑ Find $64 + 28$.

Think of the expanded form for each addend. Add.

Then add the sums.

$$8 + 4 = 10 + 2$$

Think:
Use make a ten to add the ones.

$$64 = 60 + 4$$
$$+\ 28 = 20 + 8$$
$$80 + 12 = \underline{}$$

Try This!

Use mental math to find the sum.

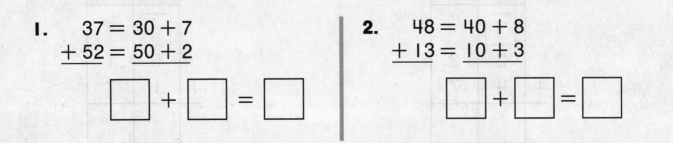

1.
$$37 = 30 + 7$$
$$+\ 52 = 50 + 2$$
$$\boxed{} + \boxed{} = \boxed{}$$

2.
$$48 = 40 + 8$$
$$+\ 13 = 10 + 3$$
$$\boxed{} + \boxed{} = \boxed{}$$

SKILL S47 — Ten Less

OBJECTIVE Find ten less than a given 2-digit number.

You can take away a ▭▭▭▭▭ from a number to find the number that is ten less.

Find ten less than 43.

STEP 1

Use 4 ▭▭▭▭▭ and 3 ▱ to show the number 43. Draw to match your ▭▭▭▭▭ ▱.

43

STEP 2

Take away 1 ▭▭▭▭▭. Draw to match your ▭▭▭▭▭ ▱. Write the number that is ten less than 43.

_____

Try This!

Write the number that is ten less.

1. 52

_____

2. 37

_____

SKILL S48 Subtract Tens

OBJECTIVE Use concrete objects to subtract tens.

You can draw a model to subtract tens.

Use ▭▭▭▭. Draw to show tens.
Subtract 50 − 20.

STEP 1 Show 5 tens. Draw the tens.	
STEP 2 Take away 2 tens. Cross them out.	5 tens − 2 tens = _____ tens
STEP 3 Write how many tens are left. Write the difference.	50 − 20 = _____

Try This!

Use ▭▭▭▭. Draw to show tens.
Write how many tens. Write the difference.

1.

7 tens − 5 tens = _____ tens

70 − 50 = _____

2.

6 tens − 1 ten = _____ tens

60 − 10 = _____

SKILL S49

Subtract Tens and Ones

OBJECTIVE Model subtracting from two-digit numbers without regrouping.

When you subtract two-digit numbers, subtract the ones and then the tens.

Subtract 27—4. Draw to show your work.

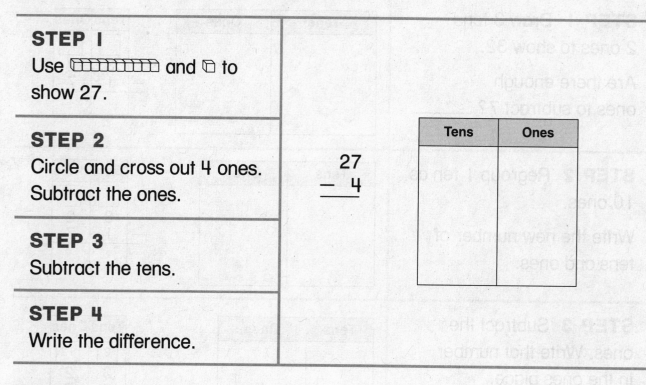

STEP 1

Use ▭▭▭▭▭▭ and ▱ to show 27.

STEP 2

Circle and cross out 4 ones. Subtract the ones.

STEP 3

Subtract the tens.

STEP 4

Write the difference.

$$27$$
$$-\ 4$$

Tens	Ones

Try This!

Use ▭▭▭▭▭▭ and ▱ to subtract. Draw to show your work. Write the difference.

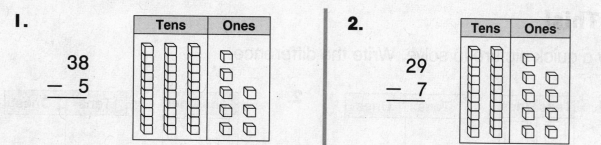

1.

$$38$$
$$-\ 5$$

Tens	Ones

2.

$$29$$
$$-\ 7$$

Tens	Ones

SKILL S50 — Model and Record 2-Digit Subtraction

OBJECTIVE Draw quick pictures and record 2-digit subtraction using the standard algorithm.

You can draw quick pictures to regroup and subtract.

Subtract 32 – 27. Draw quick pictures to solve.

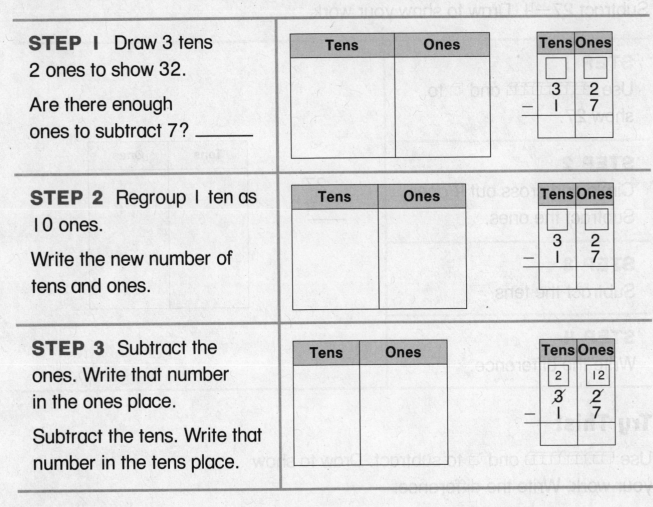

STEP 1 Draw 3 tens 2 ones to show 32.

Are there enough ones to subtract 7? _____

Tens	Ones

Tens	Ones
□ 3	□ 2
− 1	7

STEP 2 Regroup 1 ten as 10 ones.

Write the new number of tens and ones.

Tens	Ones

Tens	Ones
3	2
− 1	7

STEP 3 Subtract the ones. Write that number in the ones place.

Subtract the tens. Write that number in the tens place.

Tens	Ones

Tens	Ones
2	12
3̶	2̶
− 1	7

Try This!

Draw a quick picture to solve. Write the difference.

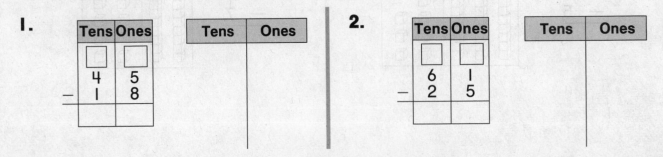

1.

Tens	Ones
□ 4	□ 5
− 1	8

Tens	Ones

2.

Tens	Ones
□ 6	□ 1
− 2	5

Tens	Ones

Name _____

SKILL S51 **Model Regrouping for Addition**

OBJECTIVE Model 2-digit addition with regrouping.

You can regroup 10 ones as 1 ten to add.

Add 15 and 37. Use ▭▭▭▭ ▭.
Draw to show your work.

STEP 1 Show 15 and 37. Use the ones to make a ten.	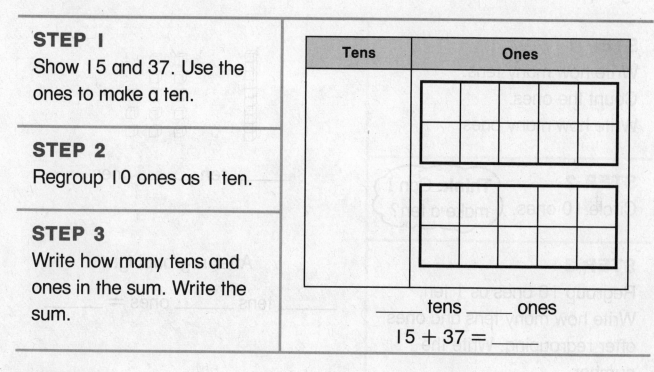
STEP 2 Regroup 10 ones as 1 ten.	
STEP 3 Write how many tens and ones in the sum. Write the sum.	

_____ tens _____ ones

15 + 37 = _____

Try This!

Use ▭▭▭▭ ▭ to regroup. Write how many
tens and ones in the sum. Write the sum.

1. Add 12 and 48.

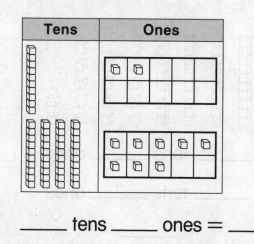

_____ tens _____ ones = _____

2. Add 37 and 35.

Tens	Ones

_____ tens _____ ones = _____

SKILL S52 Regroup Ones as Tens

OBJECTIVE Regroup ones as tens.

You can regroup 10 ones as 1 ten to make
a number.

Regroup the ones as tens. Write the number.

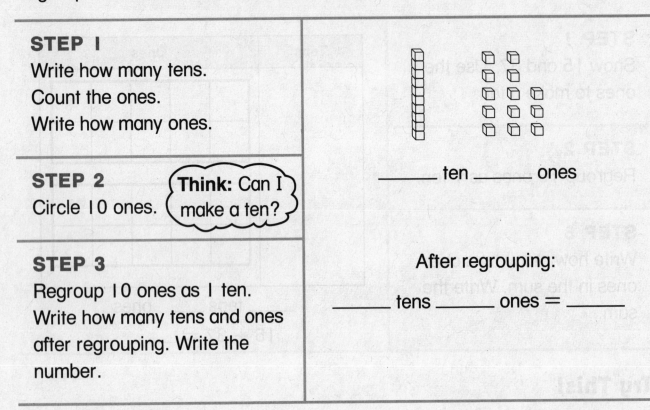

STEP 1
Write how many tens.
Count the ones.
Write how many ones.

STEP 2
Circle 10 ones.   **Think:** Can I make a ten?

STEP 3
Regroup 10 ones as 1 ten.
Write how many tens and ones
after regrouping. Write the
number.

_____ ten _____ ones

After regrouping:

_____ tens _____ ones = _____

Try This!

Write how many tens and ones. Regroup.
Write the number.

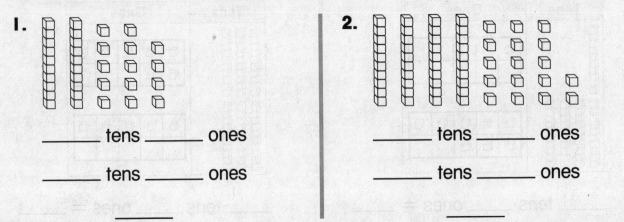

1.

_____ tens _____ ones

_____ tens _____ ones

_____

2.

_____ tens _____ ones

_____ tens _____ ones

_____

SKILL S53

Model Adding Two 2-Digit Numbers with Regrouping

OBJECTIVE Model the addition of 2-digit numbers with regrouping.

You can model 2-digit numbers to help you add.

Add 13 + 18. Draw to show your work.

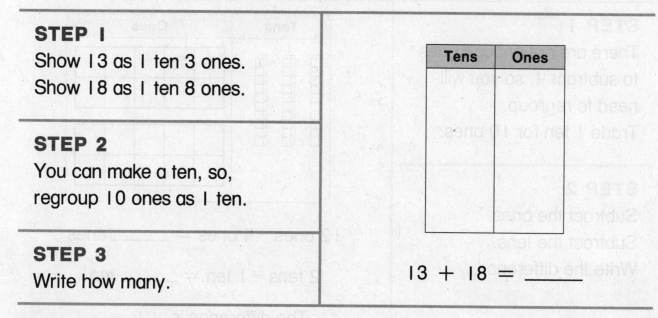

STEP 1

Show 13 as 1 ten 3 ones.
Show 18 as 1 ten 8 ones.

STEP 2

You can make a ten, so, regroup 10 ones as 1 ten.

STEP 3

Write how many.

Tens	Ones

13 + 18 = _____

Try This!

Circle **Yes** or **No**. Add.

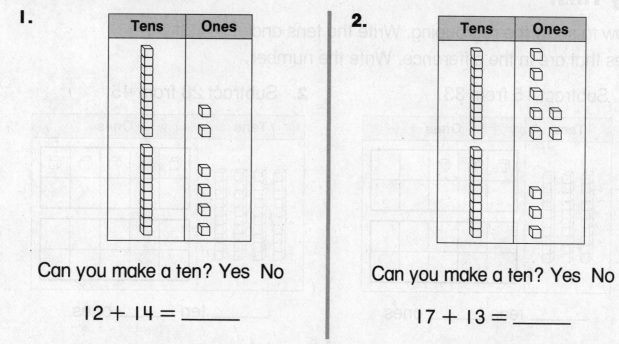

1.

Tens	Ones

Can you make a ten? Yes No

12 + 14 = _____

2.

Tens	Ones

Can you make a ten? Yes No

17 + 13 = _____

SKILL S54 **Model Regrouping for Subtraction**

OBJECTIVE Model 2-digit subtraction with regrouping.

You can trade 1 ten for 10 ones to help subtract.

Subtract 14 from 32. Draw to show your work.

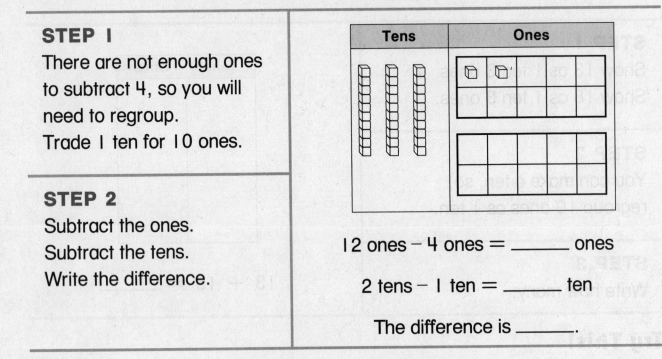

STEP 1

There are not enough ones to subtract 4, so you will need to regroup.

Trade 1 ten for 10 ones.

STEP 2

Subtract the ones.
Subtract the tens.
Write the difference.

12 ones − 4 ones = _____ ones

2 tens − 1 ten = _____ ten

The difference is _____.

Try This!

Draw to show the regrouping. Write the tens and ones that are in the difference. Write the number.

1. Subtract 15 from 33.

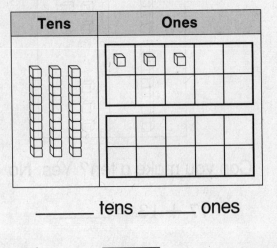

_____ tens _____ ones

_____

2. Subtract 28 from 45.

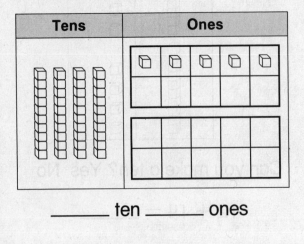

_____ ten _____ ones

_____

SKILL S55
Regroup Tens as Ones
OBJECTIVE Regroup tens as ones.

You can regroup tens as ones.

Use the number 24. Regroup 1 ten as 10 ones.
Write how many tens and ones.

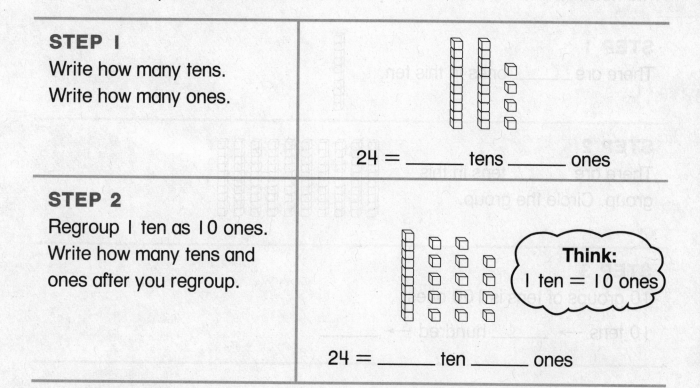

STEP 1

Write how many tens.
Write how many ones.

24 = _____ tens _____ ones

STEP 2

Regroup 1 ten as 10 ones.
Write how many tens and
ones after you regroup.

Think:
1 ten = 10 ones

24 = _____ ten _____ ones

Try This!

Regroup 1 ten as 10 ones.
Write how many tens and ones after you regroup.

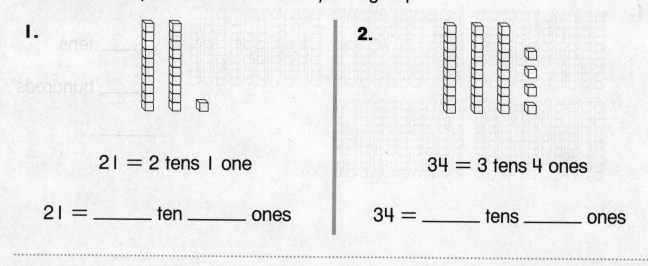

1.

21 = 2 tens 1 one

21 = _____ ten _____ ones

2.

34 = 3 tens 4 ones

34 = _____ tens _____ ones

SKILL S56

Group Tens as Hundreds

OBJECTIVE Understand that each group of 10 tens is equivalent to 1 hundred.

You can group tens as hundreds.

Circle the group of 10 tens.
Write how many hundreds. Write the number.

STEP 1

There are _____ ones in this ten.

STEP 2

There are _____ tens in this group. Circle the group.

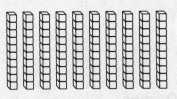

STEP 3

10 groups of tens is 100 ones.

10 tens → _____ hundred → _____

Try This!

Write how many tens. Circle groups of 10 tens.
Write how many hundreds. Write the number.

1.

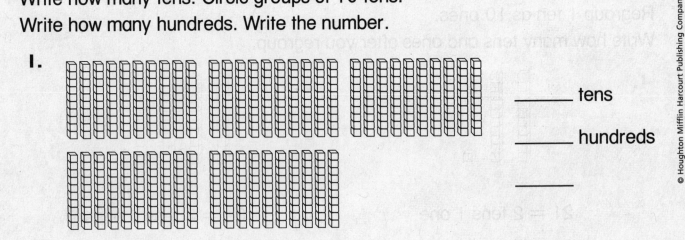

_____ tens

_____ hundreds

_____

SKILL S57

Count On and Count Back by 10 and 100

OBJECTIVE Identify 10 more, 10 less, 100 more, or 100 less than a given number.

When you count on or count back by 10 or 100, the tens digit or ones digit changes.

Write the number. Draw to show your work.

Think: Notice what digit changes.

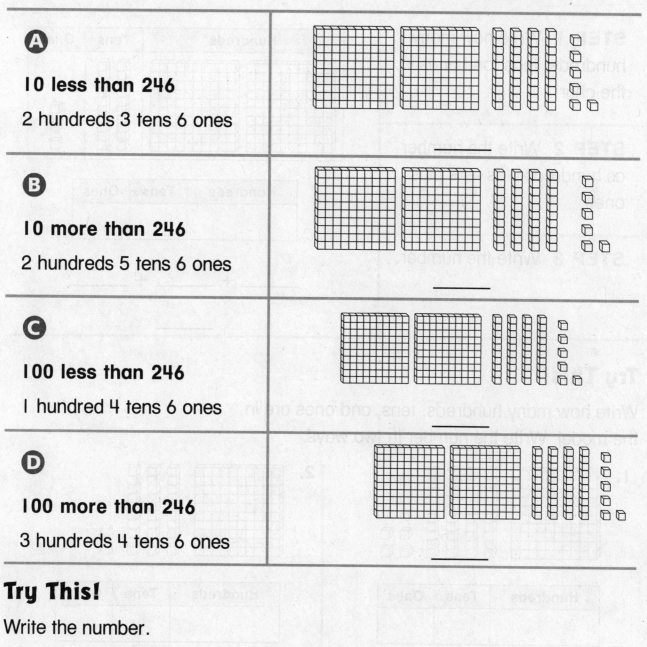

A

10 less than 246

2 hundreds 3 tens 6 ones

B

10 more than 246

2 hundreds 5 tens 6 ones

C

100 less than 246

1 hundred 4 tens 6 ones

D

100 more than 246

3 hundreds 4 tens 6 ones

Try This!

Write the number.

1. 10 less than 271

_____

2. 10 more than 271

_____

SKILL S58

Hundreds, Tens, and Ones

OBJECTIVE Apply place value concepts to write 3-digit numbers that are represented by pictorial models.

3-digit numbers have a hundreds digit, a tens digit, and a ones digit.

Write the number shown by the model.

STEP 1 Write how many hundreds, tens, and ones in the chart.	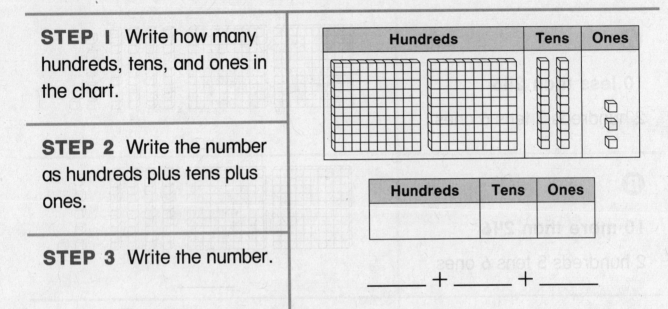
STEP 2 Write the number as hundreds plus tens plus ones.	
STEP 3 Write the number.	_____ + _____ + _____ _____

Try This!

Write how many hundreds, tens, and ones are in the model. Write the number in two ways.

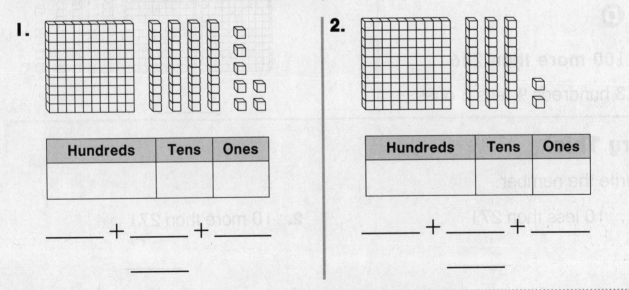

1.

Hundreds	Tens	Ones

_____ + _____ + _____

_____

2.

Hundreds	Tens	Ones

_____ + _____ + _____

_____

SKILL S59

Explore 3-Digit Numbers

OBJECTIVE Write 3-digit numbers that are represented by groups of tens.

10 tens make 1 hundred.

Write the number shown in different ways.

STEP 1

Write how many tens.

STEP 2

Circle 10 tens to make 1 hundred.

STEP 3

Write how many hundreds.
Write how many tens.

STEP 4

Write the number.

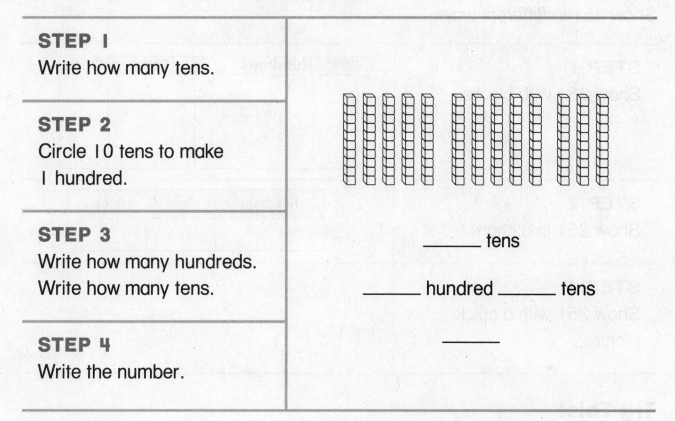

_____ tens

_____ hundred _____ tens

_____

Try This!

Circle tens to make 1 hundred.
Write the number in different ways.

1.

_____ tens

_____ hundred _____ tens

_____

2.

_____ tens

_____ hundred _____ tens

_____

SKILL S60

Model 3-Digit Numbers

OBJECTIVE Model 3-digit numbers using hundreds, tens, and ones.

You can model, or show, a number in different ways.

Show 251 in different ways.

STEP 1			
Show 251 with blocks.	**Hundreds**	**Tens**	**Ones**

STEP 2			
Show 251 in a chart.	**Hundreds**	**Tens**	**Ones**

STEP 3	
Show 251 with a quick picture.	

Try This!

Write how many hundreds, tens, and ones.
Show with ▭▭▭▭▭▭▭ and ▭.
Then draw a quick picture.

1. 234

Hundreds	Tens	Ones

2. 167

Hundreds	Tens	Ones

SKILL S61 **Draw to Represent 3-Digit Addition**

OBJECTIVE Draw quick pictures to represent 3-digit addition without regrouping.

Quick pictures that show hundreds, tens, and ones can help you add.

Add 133 and 203.

	Hundreds	Tens	Ones

STEP 1
Draw quick pictures of 133 and 203.

STEP 2
Count the hundreds, tens, and ones.

STEP 3
Write the number.

_____ hundreds _____ tens _____ ones

_____

Try This!

Draw quick pictures. Write how many hundreds, tens, and ones. Write the number.

1. Add 242 and 225.

Hundreds	Tens	Ones

_____ hundreds _____ tens

_____ ones

_____

2. Add 136 and 212.

Hundreds	Tens	Ones

_____ hundreds _____ tens

_____ ones

_____

SKILL S62 Place Value to 1,000

OBJECTIVE Use place value to describe the values of digits in numbers to 1,000

You can draw quick pictures to model place value.

Draw a quick picture to model 243.
Write the value of each digit.

STEP 1
Draw 2 hundreds.
Write the value.

STEP 2
Draw 4 tens.
Write the value.

STEP 3
Draw 3 ones.
Write the value.

243

	Hundreds	Tens	Ones
	2 hundreds	4 tens	3 ones

_____   _____   _____

Try This!

Circle the value or the meaning
of the underlined digit.

1. 4<u>3</u>9	3 hundreds	3 tens	3 ones
2. <u>7</u>27	700	70	7
3. 28<u>9</u>	9 hundreds	9 tens	9 ones
4. <u>8</u>04	8 hundreds	8 tens	8 one

SKILL S63

3-Digit Addition: Regroup Ones

OBJECTIVE Record 3-digit addition using the standard algorithm with possible regrouping of ones.

Sometimes when you add, you get 10 or more ones.

If you have 10 or more ones, regroup 10 ones as 1 ten.

Add 306 + 246.

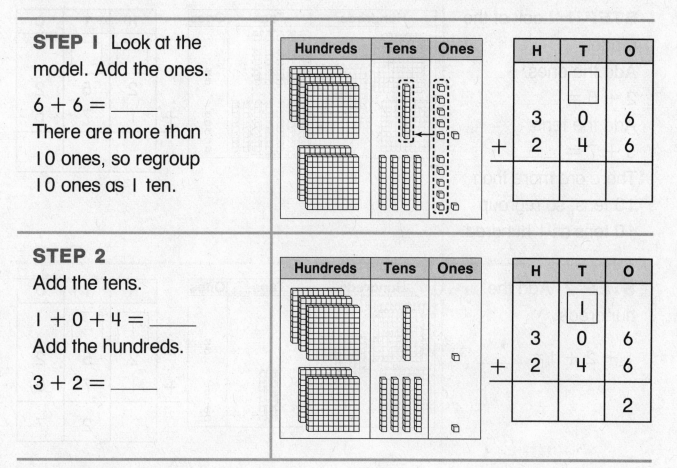

STEP 1 Look at the model. Add the ones.

$6 + 6 =$ _____

There are more than 10 ones, so regroup 10 ones as 1 ten.

H	T	O
	☐	
3	0	6
+ 2	4	6

STEP 2

Add the tens.

$1 + 0 + 4 =$ _____

Add the hundreds.

$3 + 2 =$ _____

H	T	O
	1	
3	0	6
+ 2	4	6
		2

Try This!

Write the sum.

1.

H	T	O
	☐	
5	1	8
+ 1	2	3

2.

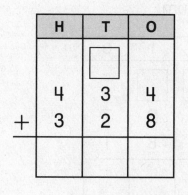

H	T	O
	☐	
4	3	4
+ 3	2	8

SKILL S64 3-Digit Addition: Regroup Tens

OBJECTIVE Record 3-digit addition using the standard algorithm with possible regrouping of tens.

If you have 10 or more tens, regroup.

Add 252 + 175.

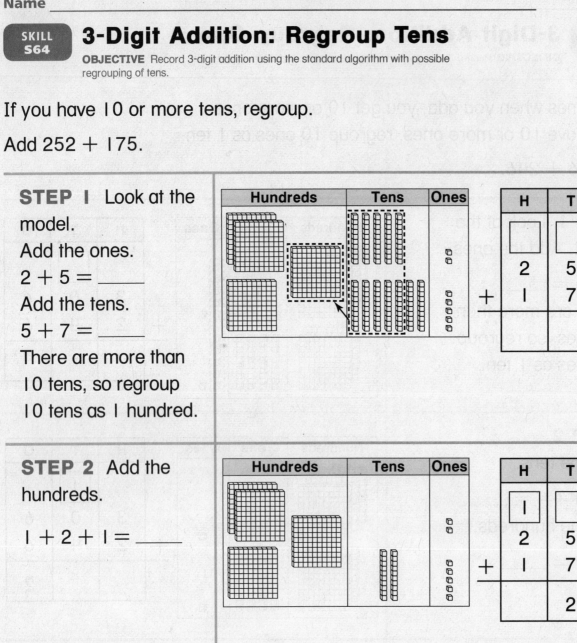

STEP 1 Look at the model.
Add the ones.
$2 + 5 = $ _____
Add the tens.
$5 + 7 = $ _____
There are more than 10 tens, so regroup 10 tens as 1 hundred.

STEP 2 Add the hundreds.

$1 + 2 + 1 = $ _____

Try This!
Write the sum.

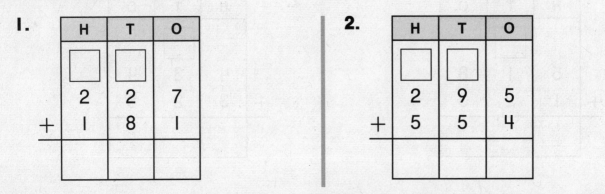

1.

H	T	O
2	2	7
+ 1	8	1

2.

H	T	O
2	9	5
+ 5	5	4

Name _____

SKILL S65

3-Digit Subtraction: Regroup Tens

OBJECTIVE Regroup 3-digit subtraction using the standard algorithm with possible regrouping of tens.

When you do not have enough ones to subtract, regroup 1 ten as 10 ones.

Subtract 353 − 138.

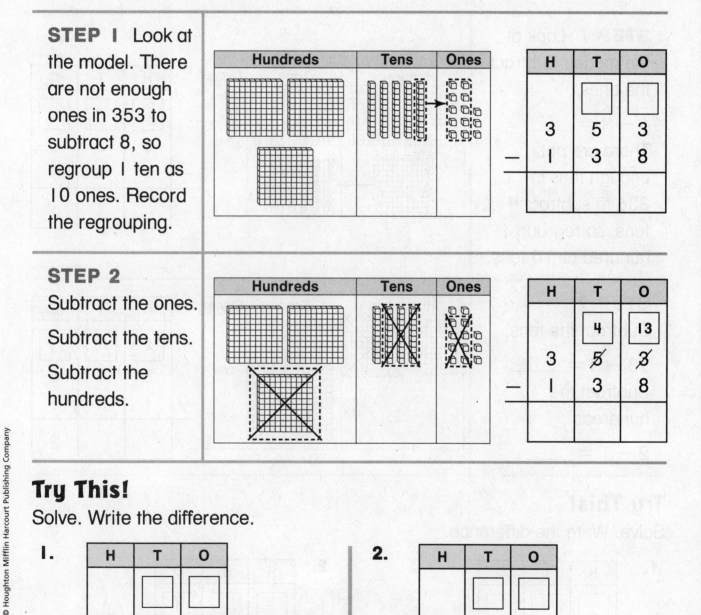

STEP 1 Look at the model. There are not enough ones in 353 to subtract 8, so regroup 1 ten as 10 ones. Record the regrouping.

H	T	O
	☐	☐
3	5	3
− 1	3	8

STEP 2
Subtract the ones.
Subtract the tens.
Subtract the hundreds.

H	T	O
	4	13
3	5̸	3̸
− 1	3	8

Try This!

Solve. Write the difference.

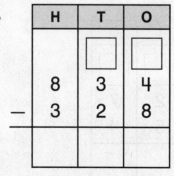

1.

H	T	O
	☐	☐
5	2	6
− 2	0	7

2.

H	T	O
	☐	☐
8	3	4
− 3	2	8

SKILL S66 3-Digit Subtraction: Regroup Hundreds

OBJECTIVE Record 3-digit subtraction with possible regrouping of hundreds.

When you do not have enough tens to subtract, regroup 1 hundred as 10 tens.

Subtract 336 − 144.

STEP 1 Look at the model. Subtract the ones.

6 − 4 = _____

There are not enough tens in 336 to subtract 4 tens, so regroup 1 hundred as 10 tens.

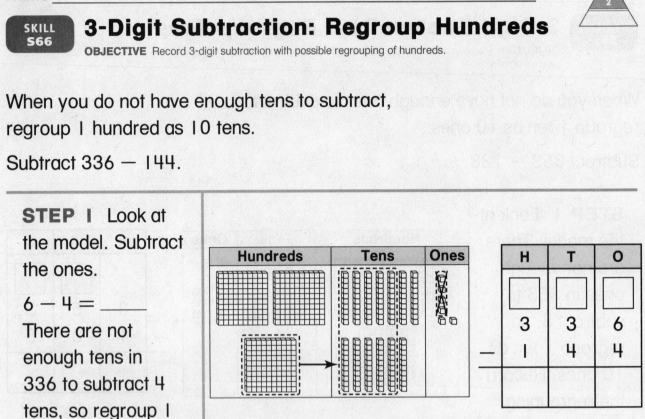

STEP 2

Subtract the tens.

13 − 4 = _____

Subtract the hundreds.

2 − 1 = _____

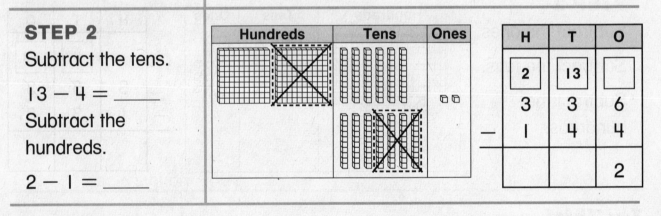

Try This!

Solve. Write the difference.

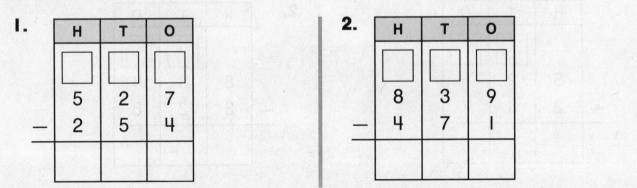

1.

H	T	O
5	2	7
− 2	5	4

2.

H	T	O
8	3	9
− 4	7	1

SKILL S67 **Identify Two-Dimensional Shapes**

OBJECTIVE Understand how to identify two-dimensional shapes, including squares and rectangles.

Shapes can be circles, triangles, rectangles, or squares.
Identify the shapes.

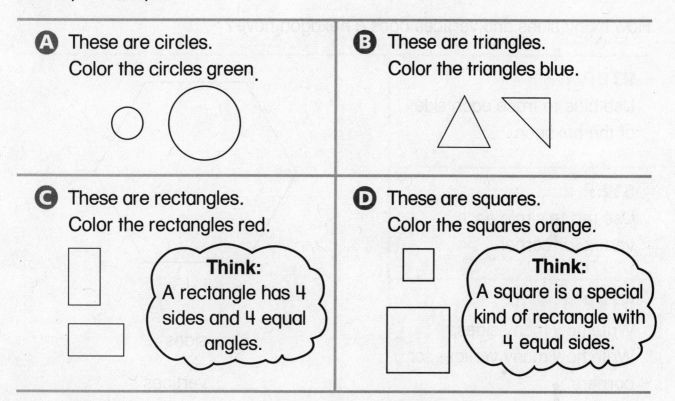

A These are circles.
Color the circles green.

B These are triangles.
Color the triangles blue.

C These are rectangles.
Color the rectangles red.

Think: A rectangle has 4 sides and 4 equal angles.

D These are squares.
Color the squares orange.

Think: A square is a special kind of rectangle with 4 equal sides.

Try This!

Color to identify the shape.

1. Color the circle green.

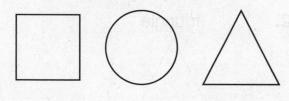

2. Color the triangle blue.

3. Color the rectangle red.

4. Color the square orange.

Describe Two-Dimensional Shapes

OBJECTIVE Describe attributes of two-dimensional shapes.

You can describe a shape by telling how many sides or vertices it has.

How many sides and vertices does a hexagon have?

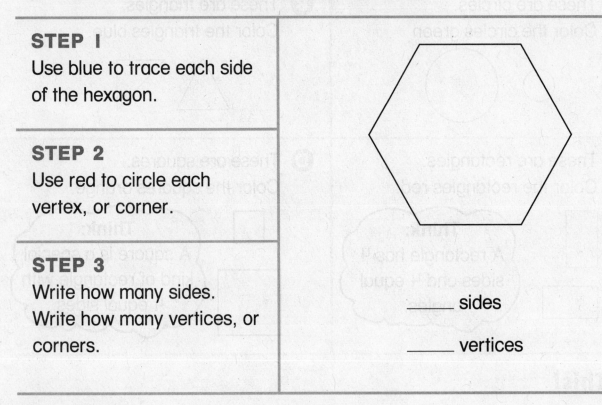

STEP 1
Use blue to trace each side of the hexagon.

STEP 2
Use red to circle each vertex, or corner.

STEP 3
Write how many sides.
Write how many vertices, or corners.

_____ sides

_____ vertices

Try This!

Write the number of sides and vertices.

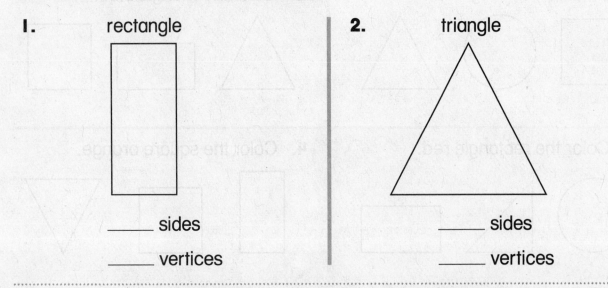

I.   rectangle

_____ sides

_____ vertices

2.   triangle

_____ sides

_____ vertices

SKILL S69

Sort and Classify Two-Dimensional Shapes

OBJECTIVE Sort and classify two-dimensional shapes by color and size.

You can sort shapes by color and size.

Sort the shapes by color and by size.

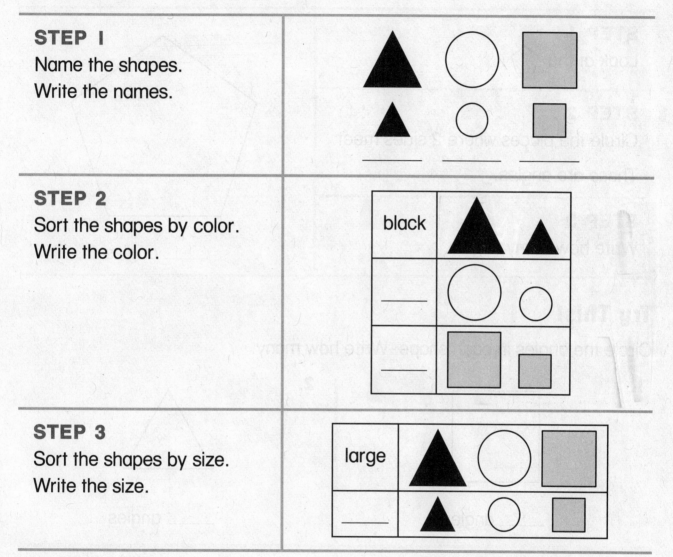

STEP 1

Name the shapes.
Write the names.

STEP 2

Sort the shapes by color.
Write the color.

STEP 3

Sort the shapes by size.
Write the size.

Try This!

1. Look at the large shapes.

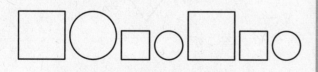

Write how many. _____

2. Look at the gray shapes.

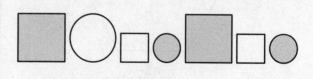

Write how many. _____

© Houghton Mifflin Harcourt Publishing Company

SKILL S70   # Angles in Two-Dimensional Shapes

OBJECTIVE Identify angles in two-dimensional shapes.

An **angle** is where 2 sides meet.

How many angles does a ⬠ have?

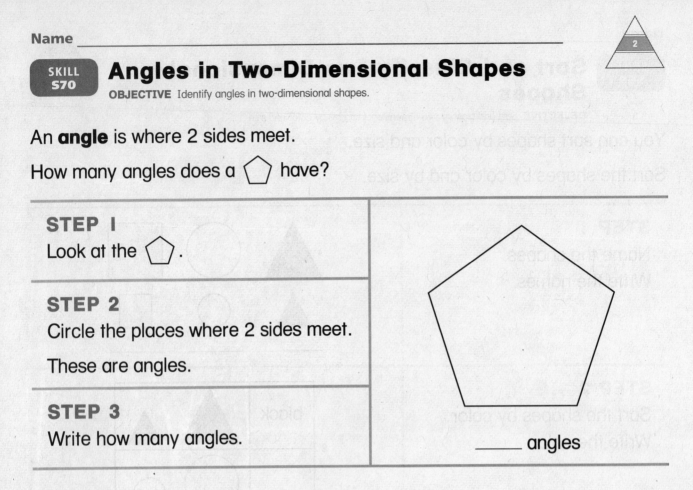

STEP 1 Look at the ⬠.	
STEP 2 Circle the places where 2 sides meet. These are angles.	
STEP 3 Write how many angles.	____ angles

Try This!

Circle the angles in each shape. Write how many.

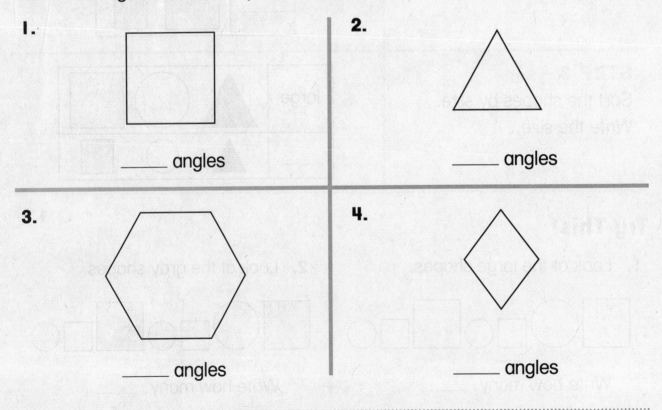

I.

____ angles

2.

____ angles

3.

____ angles

4.

____ angles

Name _____

Identify Cones, Cylinders, and Spheres

OBJECTIVE Identify three-dimensional shapes, including cones, cylinders, and spheres.

You can identify cones, cylinders, and spheres by their shapes.

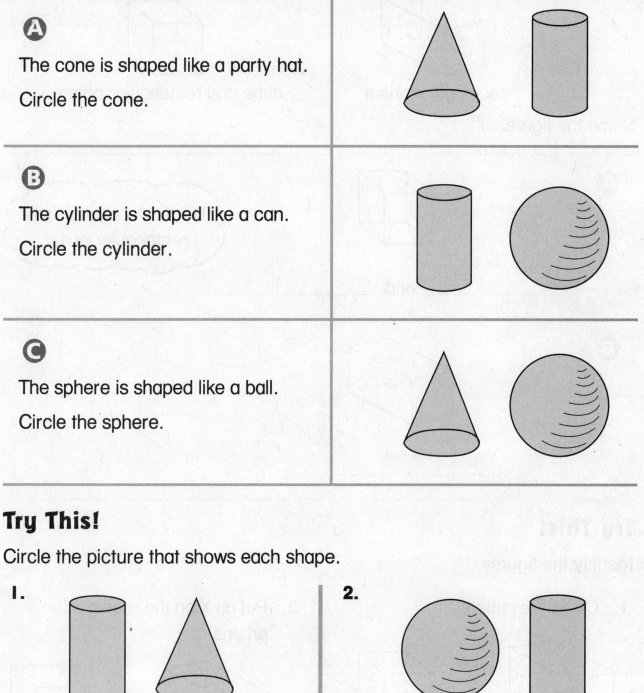

A

The cone is shaped like a party hat.

Circle the cone.

B

The cylinder is shaped like a can.

Circle the cylinder.

C

The sphere is shaped like a ball.

Circle the sphere.

Try This!

Circle the picture that shows each shape.

I.

cone

2.

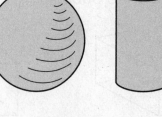

sphere

SKILL S72

Identify Rectangular Prisms and Cubes

OBJECTIVE Identify rectangular prisms and cubes by shape.

Rectangular prisms and cubes have sides that are rectangles. The sides of a cube are all the same.

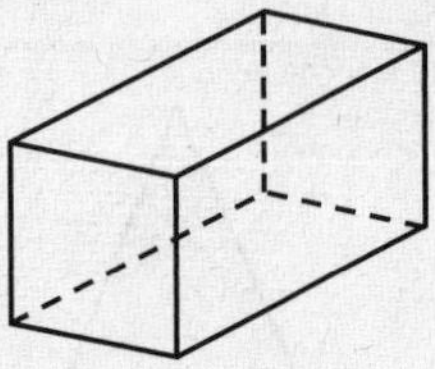

rectangular prism

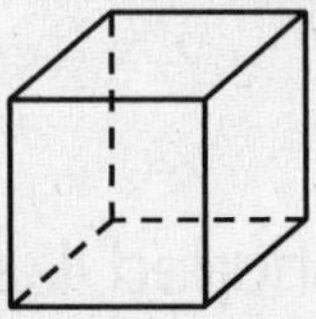

cube and rectangular prism

Name the figure.

A

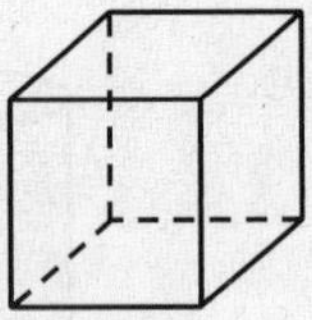

Think: A cube is also a rectangular prism.

_____ and _____

B

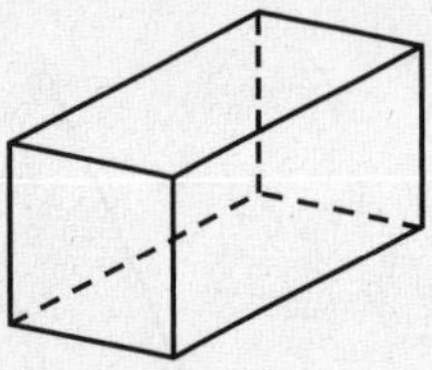

_____

Try This!

Identify the figures.

1. Circle the cube.

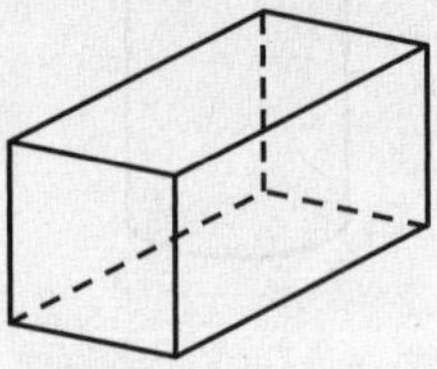

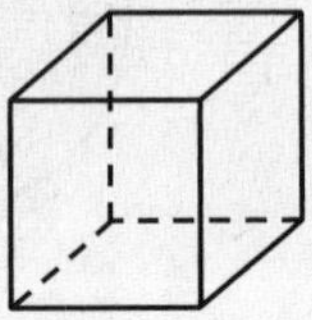

2. Put an X on the rectangular prisms.

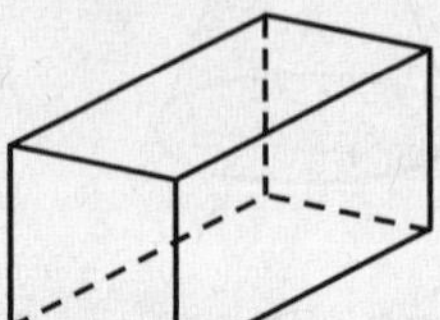

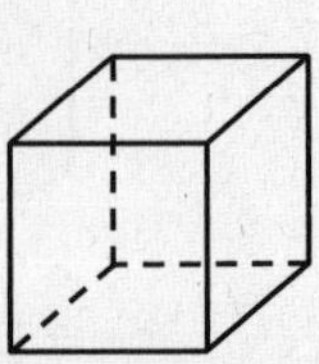

© Houghton Mifflin Harcourt Publishing Company

SKILL S73 **Equal Parts**

OBJECTIVE Identify regions that are separated into equal and unequal parts.

Shapes can show equal or unequal parts.

A Equal parts are the same size.

Shade 1 part of the circle to show equal parts.

B Unequal parts are not the same size.

Shade 1 part of the circle to show unequal parts.

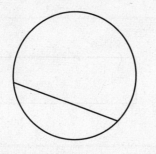

Try This!

Circle **equal parts** or **unequal parts**.

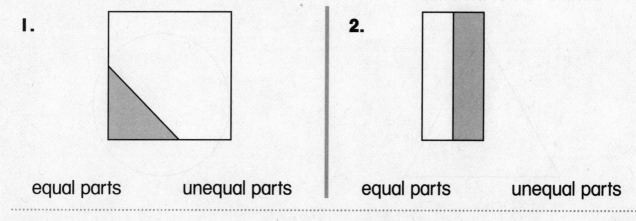

1.	2.
equal parts unequal parts	equal parts unequal parts

SKILL S74

Describe Equal Parts

OBJECTIVE Identify and describe one equal part as a half of, a third of, or a fourth of a whole.

You can show a half, a third, and a fourth
by showing equal parts of a figure.

Draw to show equal parts.
Color one of the equal parts.

A

Draw a line to show halves.
Color a half of the rectangle.

B

Draw lines to show thirds.
Color a third of the rectangle.

C

Draw lines to show fourths.
Color a fourth of the rectangle.

Try This!

I. Draw a line to show halves.
Color a half of the shape.

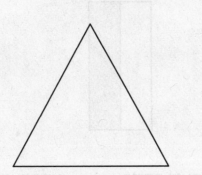

2. Draw lines to show fourths.
Color a fourth of the shape.

Name _____

SKILL S75 # Show Equal Parts of a Whole
OBJECTIVE Partition shapes to show halves, thirds, or fourths.

You can show halves, thirds, or fourths by showing equal parts of a whole.

You can draw lines to show equal parts.

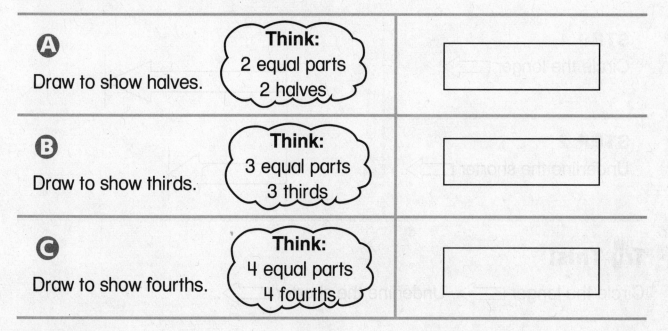

A

Draw to show halves.

Think:
2 equal parts
2 halves

B

Draw to show thirds.

Think:
3 equal parts
3 thirds

C

Draw to show fourths.

Think:
4 equal parts
4 fourths

Try This!

Draw to show equal parts.

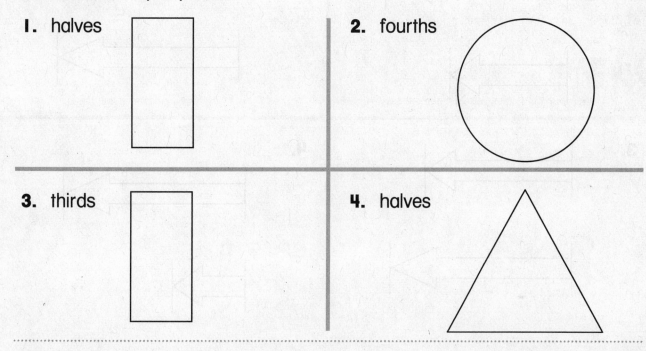

1. halves

2. fourths

3. thirds

4. halves

SKILL S76

Compare Length

OBJECTIVE Compare lengths of objects.

You can compare the lengths of two objects to tell if one is longer or shorter.

Which 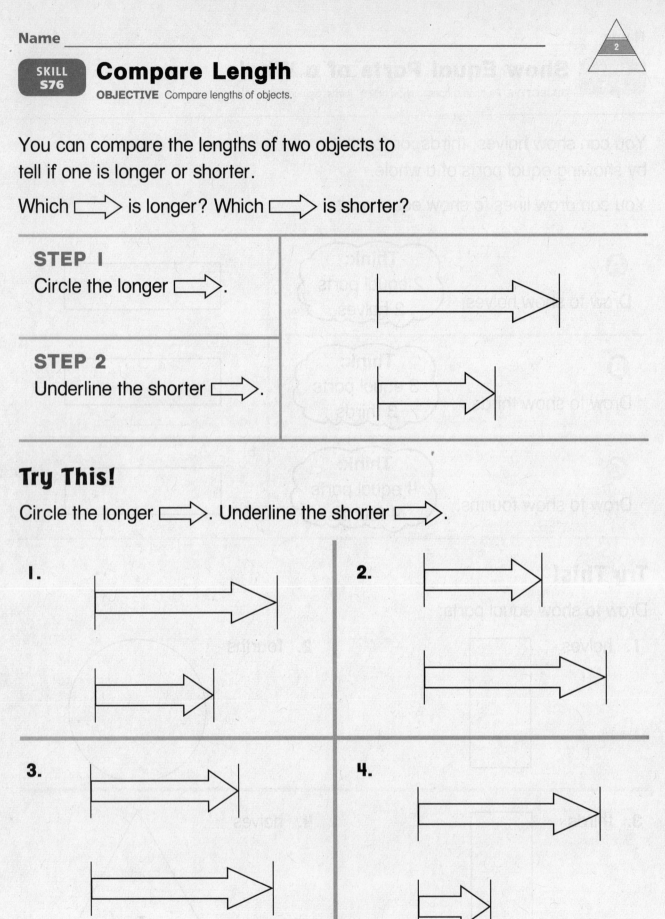 is longer? Which ⇒ is shorter?

STEP 1
Circle the longer ⇒.

STEP 2
Underline the shorter ⇒.

Try This!

Circle the longer ⇒. Underline the shorter ⇒.

1.

2.

3.

4.

Name _____

SKILL S77   **Order Length**

OBJECTIVE Order three objects by length.

To order objects by length, compare them.
Find the shortest and the longest objects.

Are the ⇨ in order from shortest to longest
as you go from the top to the bottom?

STEP 1
Compare the ⇨.

STEP 2
Is the shortest ⇨ on the top? _____

STEP 3
Is the longest ⇨ on the bottom? _____

STEP 4
Are the ⇨ in order? _____

Try This!

Circle the ⇨ if they are in order from shortest
to longest as you go from the top to the bottom.
Draw an X on the ⇨ if they are not in order.

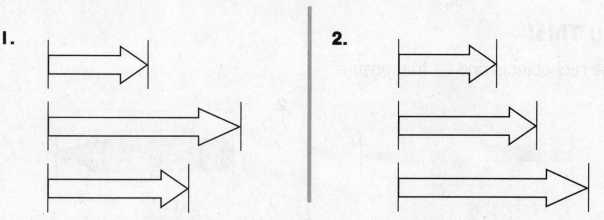

1.

2.

SKILL S78

Use Nonstandard Units to Measure Length

OBJECTIVE Use nonstandard units to measure the length of objects.

You can use ▧ to measure the length of an object.

About how many ▧ long is the ribbon?

Draw to show your work.

STEP 1 Set one ▧ below one end of the object you are measuring.	
STEP 2 Place more ▧ until you reach the other end of the ribbon.	
STEP 3 Count how many ▧. Write how many.	about _____ ▧

Try This!

Use real objects and ▧ to measure.

1.

about _____ ▧

2.

about _____ ▧

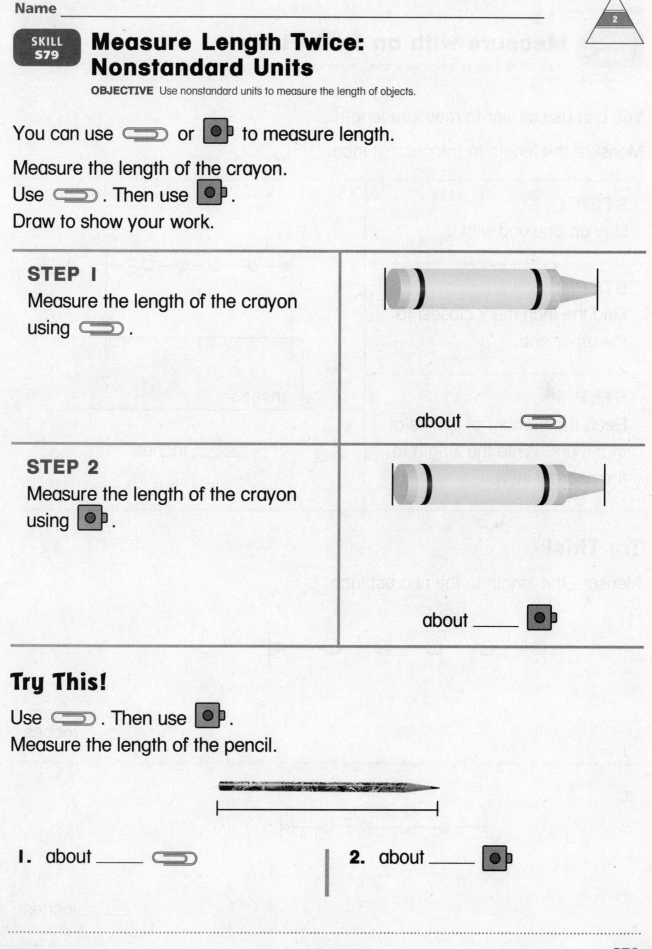

SKILL S79

Measure Length Twice: Nonstandard Units

OBJECTIVE Use nonstandard units to measure the length of objects.

You can use ⬭ or ⬛ to measure length.

Measure the length of the crayon.
Use ⬭ . Then use ⬛ .
Draw to show your work.

STEP 1

Measure the length of the crayon using ⬭ .

about _____ ⬭

STEP 2

Measure the length of the crayon using ⬛ .

about _____ ⬛

Try This!

Use ⬭ . Then use ⬛ .
Measure the length of the pencil.

1. about _____ ⬭   **2.** about _____ ⬛

SKILL S80 **Measure with an Inch Ruler**

OBJECTIVE Measure the lengths of objects to the nearest inch using an inch ruler.

You can use a ruler to measure length.

Measure the length to the nearest inch.

STEP 1 Line up one end with 0.	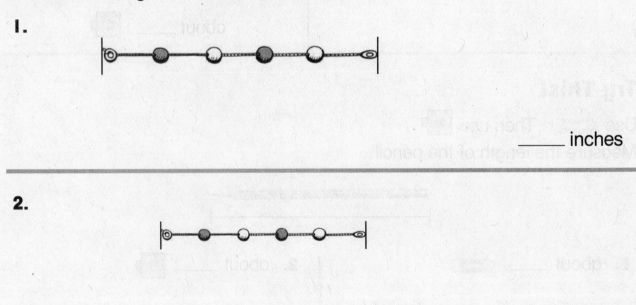
STEP 2 Find the inch mark closest to the other end.	
STEP 3 Read the number of inches at that mark. Write the length to the nearest inch.	_____ inches

Try This!

Measure the length to the nearest inch.

1.

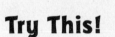

_____ inches

2.

_____ inches

SKILL S81 — Estimate Lengths in Inches

OBJECTIVE Estimate the lengths of objects by mentally partitioning the lengths into inches.

You can estimate length of an object to the nearest inch.

The bead is 1 inch long.
Estimate the length of the string in inches.

STEP 1 Write how many beads will fit on the string.	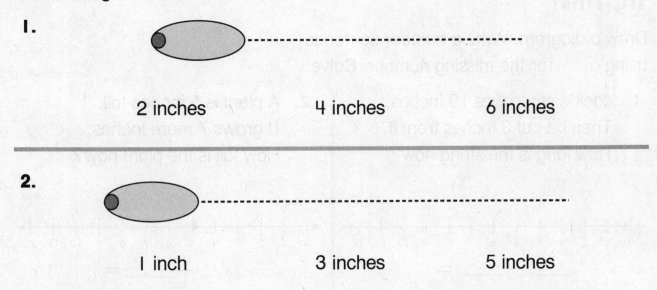
STEP 2 Write the length of the string in inches. **Think:** Each bead is 1 inch long.	_____ beads will fit on the string. The string is about _____ inches long.

Try This!

Circle the best estimate for the length of the string.

1.

2 inches   4 inches   6 inches

2.

1 inch   3 inches   5 inches

SKILL S82

Add and Subtract in Inches

OBJECTIVE Solve addition and subtraction problems involving the lengths of objects by using the strategy *draw a diagram*.

You can use a number line to add or subtract inches.

Deb has two ribbons. One ribbon is 7 inches long.
The other ribbon is 4 inches long.
How many inches of ribbon does Deb have?

STEP 1

Use the number line to draw a diagram. Draw from 0 to 7 to show the first ribbon. Draw 4 more units to show the other ribbon.

↤+++++++++++++↦
0 1 2 3 4 5 6 7 8 9 10 11 12

STEP 2

Write an addition sentence using a ☐ for the missing number.

_____ + _____ = ☐

STEP 3

Solve. Write how many inches of ribbon Deb has.

Deb has _____ inches of ribbon.

Try This!

Draw a diagram. Write a number sentence using a ☐ for the missing number. Solve.

1. Jack's string was 10 inches.
   Then he cut 3 inches from it.
   How long is the string now?

   ↤+++++++++++++↦
   0 1 2 3 4 5 6 7 8 9 10 11 12

   _____ − _____ = ☐

   The string is _____ inches long.

2. A plant is 5 inches tall.
   It grows 7 more inches.
   How tall is the plant now?

   ↤+++++++++++++↦
   0 1 2 3 4 5 6 7 8 9 10 11 12

   _____ + _____ = ☐

   The plant is _____ inches tall.

SKILL S83
Measure with a Centimeter Model
OBJECTIVE Use concrete objects to measure length in centimeters.

You can use a centimeter model to measure the length of an object.

Measure the length in centimeters.

STEP 1 Place unit cubes under the glue stick. Count.	
STEP 2 Write how many unit cubes long the glue stick is.	

The glue stick is about _____ unit cubes long.

So, the glue stick is about _____ centimeters long.

STEP 3
Write how many centimeters long the glue stick is.
Think: Each unit cube is about 1 centimeter long.

Try This!

Use unit cubes.
Measure the length in centimeters.

1.

about _____ centimeters

2.

about _____ centimeters

SKILL S84

Measure with a Centimeter Ruler

OBJECTIVE Measure lengths of objects to the nearest centimeter using a centimeter ruler.

You can use a centimeter ruler to measure length of an object to the nearest centimeter.

Measure the ribbon's length to the nearest centimeter.

STEP 1

Line up the left end of the ribbon with the zero mark on the ruler.

STEP 2

Find the centimeter mark closest to the other end of the ribbon.

STEP 3

Write the length to the nearest centimeter.

The ribbon is about _____ centimeters long.

Try This!

Measure the length to the nearest centimeter.

1.

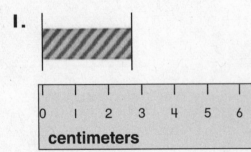

_____ centimeters

2.

_____ centimeters

© Houghton Mifflin Harcourt Publishing Company

SKILL S85

Centimeters and Meters

OBJECTIVE Measure the lengths of objects in both centimeters and meters to explore the inverse relationship between size and number of units.

You can measure shorter lengths in centimeters and longer lengths in meters.

1 meter is the same as 100 centimeters.

Measure to the nearest centimeter.
Then measure to the nearest meter.

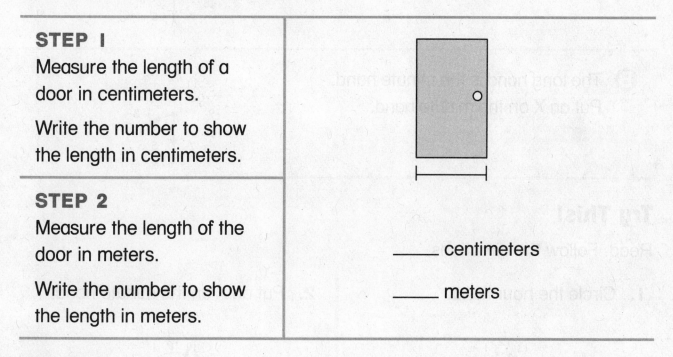

STEP 1

Measure the length of a door in centimeters.

Write the number to show the length in centimeters.

STEP 2

Measure the length of the door in meters.

Write the number to show the length in meters.

_____ centimeters

_____ meters

Try This!

Measure the real object to the nearest centimeter.
Then measure to the nearest meter.

1. window

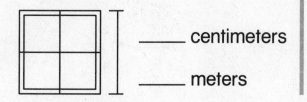

_____ centimeters

_____ meters

2. chalkboard

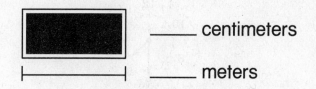

_____ centimeters

_____ meters

SKILL S86

Identify Hands on an Analog Clock

OBJECTIVE Identify the minute hand and the hour hand on an analog clock.

An **analog clock** has a minute hand
and an hour hand.

A The short hand is the hour hand.
Circle the hour hand.

B The long hand is the minute hand.
Put an X on the minute hand.

Try This!

Read. Follow the directions.

1. Circle the hour hand.

2. Put an X on the minute hand.

---

3. Circle the hour hand.

4. Put an X on the minute hand.

© Houghton Mifflin Harcourt Publishing Company

SKILL S87

Match Times to the Hour on an Analog and a Digital Clock

OBJECTIVE Match times to the hour on analog and digital clocks.

There are different kinds of clocks.

Each clock below shows the same time.
Write the time two ways.

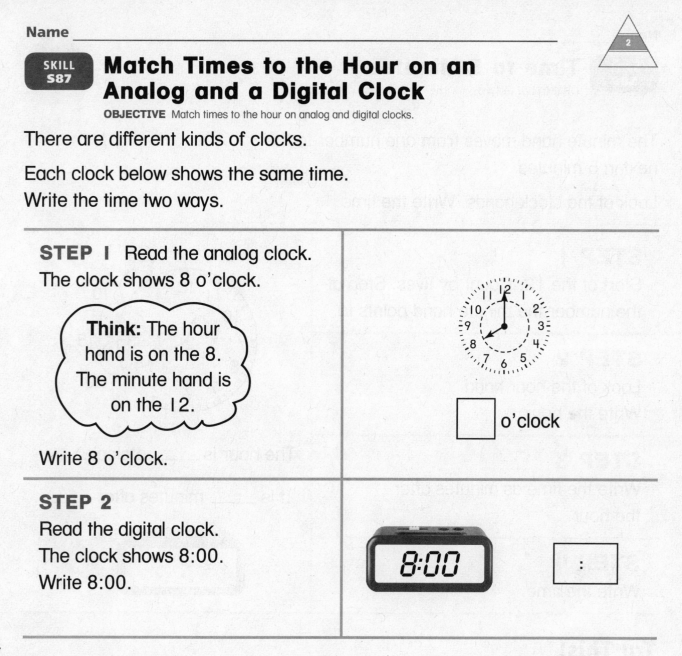

STEP 1 Read the analog clock.
The clock shows 8 o'clock.

Think: The hour hand is on the 8. The minute hand is on the 12.

Write 8 o'clock.

☐ o'clock

STEP 2
Read the digital clock.
The clock shows 8:00.
Write 8:00.

8:00

☐ : ☐

Try This!

Circle the clock that shows the same time.

1.

3:00   9:00

2.

10:00

Name _____

SKILL S88 — Time to 5 Minutes

OBJECTIVE Tell and write time to the nearest five minutes.

The minute hand moves from one number to the next in 5 minutes.

Look at the clock hands. Write the time.

STEP 1
Start at the 12. Count by fives. Stop at the number the minute hand points to.

STEP 2
Look at the hour hand.
Write the hour.

STEP 3
Write the time as minutes after the hour.

STEP 4
Write the time.

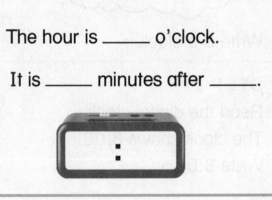

The hour is _____ o'clock.

It is _____ minutes after _____.

Try This!

Look at the clock hands. Write the time.

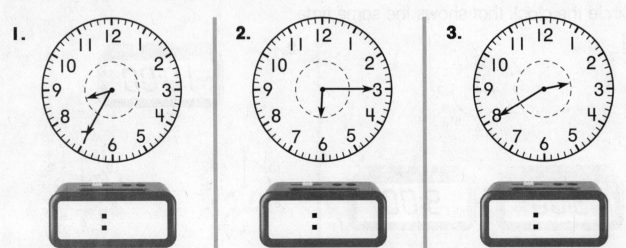

1.　　2.　　3.

S88   Skill S88

SKILL S89 — Pennies and Dimes

OBJECTIVE Solve word problems determining the value of a group of pennies or a group of dimes.

A penny is worth 1 cent.

A dime is worth 10 cents.

Use or ⬤ . Draw them. Count by ones or count by tens. Write the total amount.

A Joe has 4 pennies. How many cents does he have?

☐ ¢

B Ana has 3 dimes. How many cents does she have?

☐ ¢

Try This!

Draw 🪙 or draw ⬤ . Count by ones or count by tens. Write the total amount.

1. Dillon has 2 pennies. How many cents does he have?

☐ ¢

2. Suri has 2 dimes. How many cents does she have?

☐ ¢

SKILL S90 **Identify the Value of a Nickel and a Dime**

OBJECTIVE Count nickels and dimes and write the values.

A nickel is worth 5¢. A dime is worth 10¢.

Count the nickels and dimes.
Write how many cents.

A Jim has 3 nickels. How many cents does Jim have?

Think: Count by 5s.

☐ ¢

B Marla has 2 dimes. How many cents does Marla have?

Think: Count by 10s.

☐ ¢

Try This!

Count the coins. Write how many cents.

1. Andy finds 3 dimes. How many cents does Andy find?

☐ ¢

2. Karen has 2 nickels. How many cents does Karen have?

☐ ¢

SKILL S91

One Dollar

OBJECTIVE Solve problems involving one dollar, using $ and ¢ symbols appropriately.

One dollar has the same value as 100 cents.
You can write one dollar as $1.00.

Circle coins to make $1.00.
Cross out the coins you do not use.

STEP 1 Count on to 100¢. Circle the coins to make $1.00. **STEP 2** Cross out the coins you do not use.	

Try This!

Circle coins to make $1.00.
Cross out the coins you do not use.

1.

2.

Name _____

SKILL S92 **Amounts Greater than $1**

OBJECTIVE Find and record the total value for money amounts greater than $1.

You can count on to find amounts greater than $1.00.

Find the total value of the coins.

| **STEP 1** Count on and circle the coins that make one dollar. |
| **STEP 2** Count on from $1.00 to find the total value of the coins. |
| **STEP 3** Write the total value as a dollar amount. |

_____ _____ _____

Total value: _____

Try This!

Circle the coins that make $1.00.

Then write the total value of the money shown.

1. _____

2. _____

SKILL S93 Read Picture Graphs

OBJECTIVE Interpret data shown in a picture graph.

You can use a **picture graph** to show how many.

Read the picture graph.

STEP 1
Circle the title.
This is what the graph shows.

STEP 2
Underline the sentence that
tells what each ⅄ stands for.

Colors We Like				
blue	⅄	⅄	⅄	
red	⅄	⅄	⅄	⅄

Each ⅄ stands for 1 child.

STEP 3
Count the ⅄ in each row.
Write the number for each color
on the line.

_____ children like blue.

_____ children like red.

Try This!

Use the picture graph to answer the questions.

Favorite Fruits				
banana	⅄	⅄	⅄	⅄
grape	⅄	⅄		

Each ⅄ stands for 1 child.

1. How many children chose
   banana?

   _____ children

2. Which fruit did more children
   choose? Circle.

   banana   grape

SKILL S94 — Make Tally Charts

OBJECTIVE Organize, represent, and interpret data in tally charts.

A **tally chart** uses tally marks to show how many.

Make a tally chart to show how many of each shape.

STEP 1
Mark a tally mark for each heart.

STEP 2
Mark a tally mark for each circle.

STEP 3
Mark a tally mark for each square.

STEP 4
Write the number of hearts, circles, and squares.

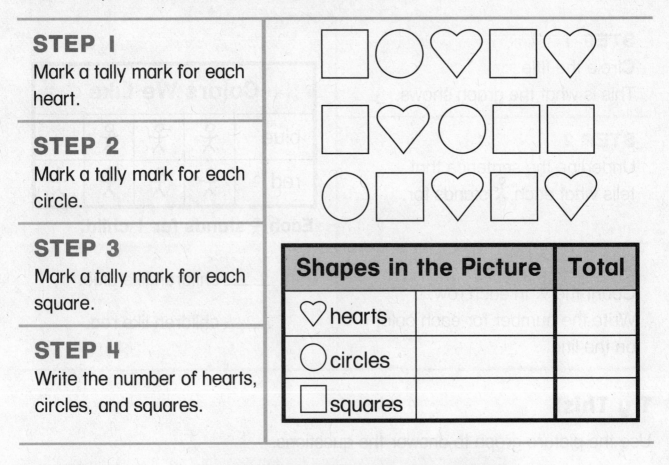

Shapes in the Picture		Total
♡ hearts		
○ circles		
☐ squares		

Try This!

Use the tally chart.

Favorite Color		Total
yellow	⊬⊬⊬ |||	
green	⊬⊬⊬		

1. Write the totals in the tally chart above.

2. Circle the color that was chosen by fewer children.

yellow   green

SKILL S95 · Read Bar Graphs

OBJECTIVE Interpret data in bar graphs.

You can read bar graphs by comparing the lengths of the bars.

Use the bar graph below about circle colors.
How many red circles are there?

STEP 1

Look at the number below the right end of the bar for red. Circle the number.

STEP 2

Write the number that tells how many red circles.

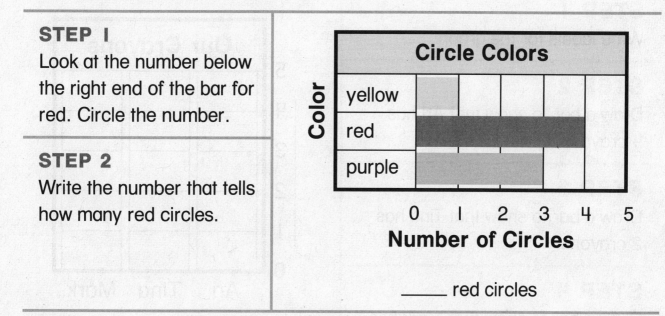

_____ red circles

Try This!

Use the bar graph to answer the questions.

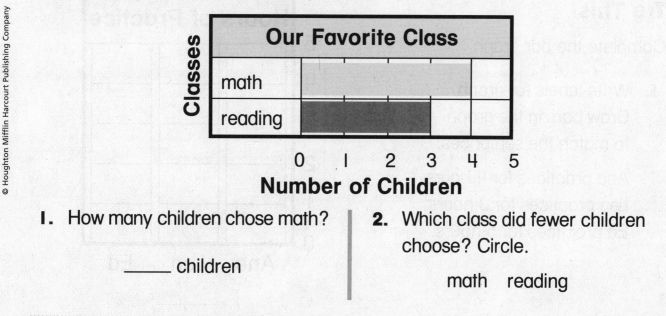

1. How many children chose math?

   _____ children

2. Which class did fewer children choose? Circle.

   math   reading

SKILL S96

Make Bar Graphs

OBJECTIVE Draw a bar graph to represent a data set.

A **bar graph** uses bars to show how many.

Make a bar graph to show how many crayons each child has.

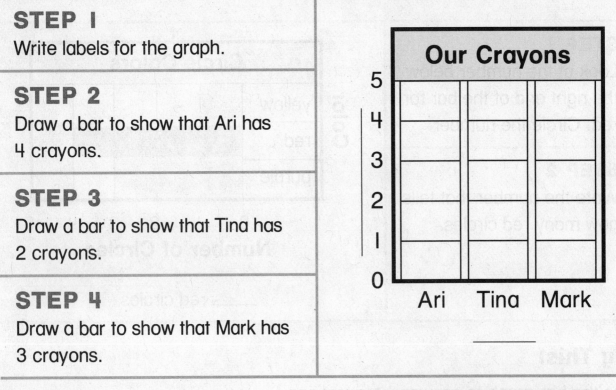

STEP 1
Write labels for the graph.

STEP 2
Draw a bar to show that Ari has 4 crayons.

STEP 3
Draw a bar to show that Tina has 2 crayons.

STEP 4
Draw a bar to show that Mark has 3 crayons.

Our Crayons

Ari   Tina   Mark

_____

Try This!

Complete the bar graph.

1. Write labels for graph.
Draw bars in the graph
to match the sentences.

Ana practices for 4 hours.
Len practices for 3 hours.
Ed practices for 5 hours.

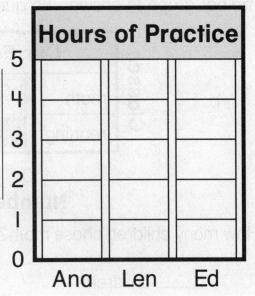

Hours of Practice

Ana   Len   Ed

_____

EXAMPLE E1

Same Number

There is a set of 3 roses. There is a set of 3 vases.
How can you show that there are the same number of roses and vases?

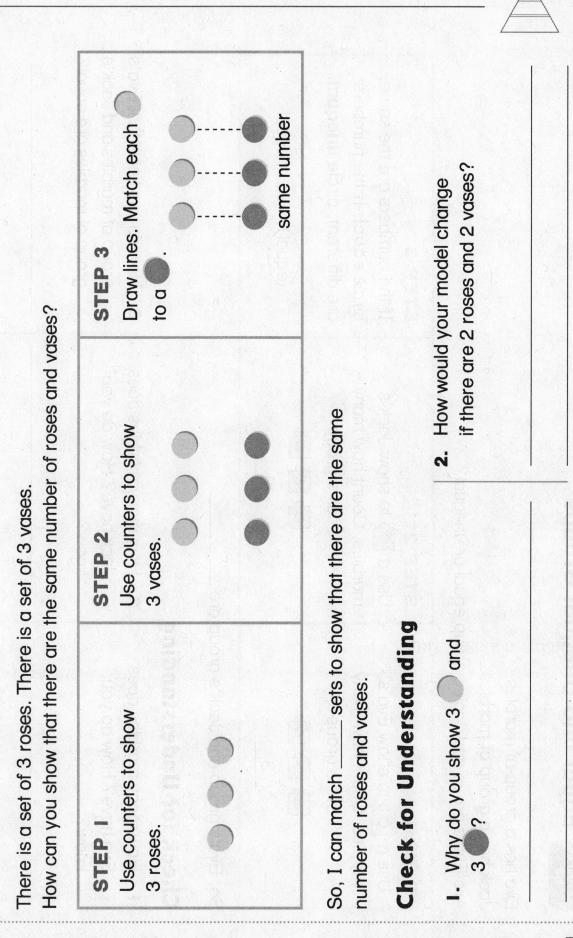

STEP 1

Use counters to show 3 roses.

STEP 2

Use counters to show 3 vases.

STEP 3

Draw lines. Match each _____ to a _____.

same number

So, I can match _____ sets to show that there are the same number of roses and vases.

Check for Understanding

1. Why do you show 3 _____ and 3 _____?

2. How would your model change if there are 2 roses and 2 vases?

EXAMPLE E2   Equal and Unequal Groups

Eva has a group of marbles.
Jack has a group of marbles.
Are Eva's group and Jack's group equal or unequal?

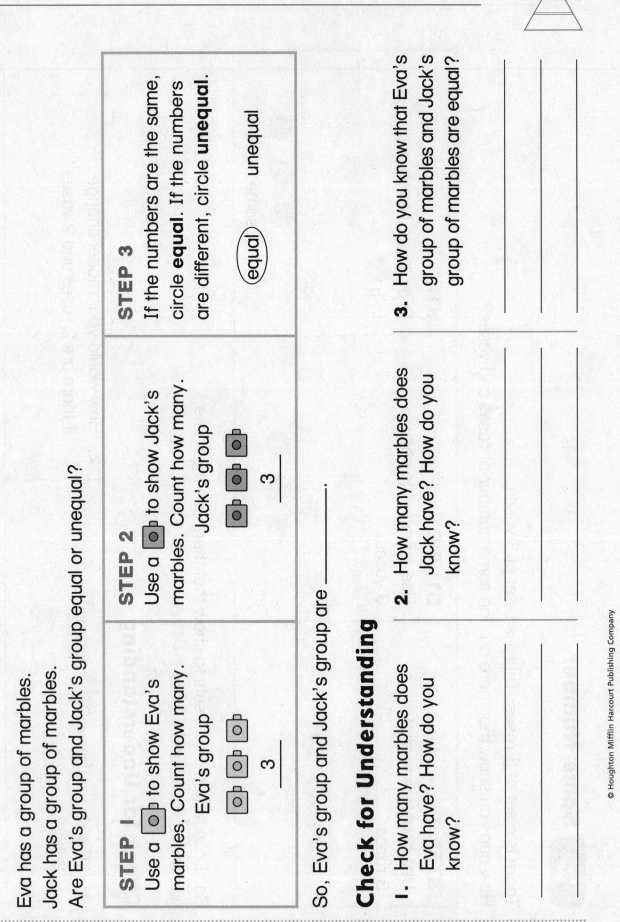

STEP 1

Use a 🔲 to show Eva's marbles. Count how many.

Eva's group

___3___

STEP 2

Use a 🔲 to show Jack's marbles. Count how many.

Jack's group

___3___

STEP 3

If the numbers are the same, circle **equal**. If the numbers are different, circle **unequal**.

(equal)   unequal

So, Eva's group and Jack's group are _____.

Check for Understanding

1. How many marbles does Eva have? How do you know?

_____
_____
_____

2. How many marbles does Jack have? How do you know?

_____
_____
_____

3. How do you know that Eva's group of marbles and Jack's group of marbles are equal?

_____
_____
_____

© Houghton Mifflin Harcourt Publishing Company

Name ____________________

EXAMPLE E3 Count and Write Numbers to 10

Dillon counts his toys. He has 3 toys.
How can he show and write the number of toys?

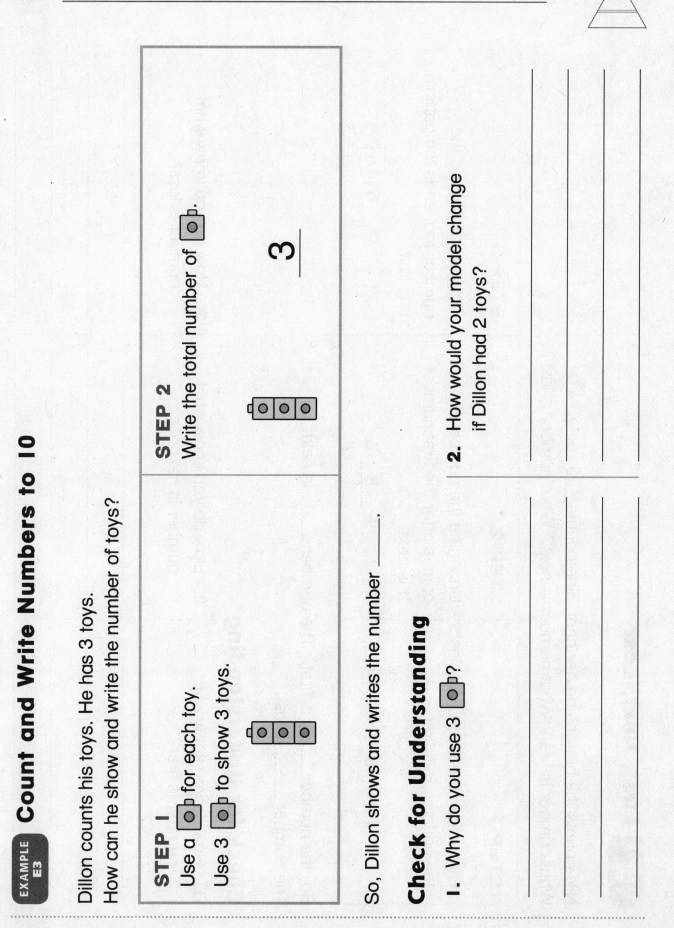

STEP 1
Use a cube for each toy.
Use 3 cubes to show 3 toys.

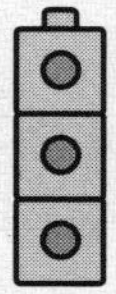

STEP 2
Write the total number of cubes.

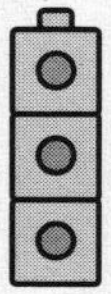

3

So, Dillon shows and writes the number ____.

Check for Understanding

1. Why do you use 3 cubes?

2. How would your model change if Dillon had 2 toys?

EXAMPLE E4

First, Next, Last

Niki counts the buttons on her coat. She counts 4, 5, 6.
What number is first? What number is next? What number is last?

STEP 1	STEP 2	STEP 3
Circle the number that begins the pattern. It is first.	Underline the number that comes after the first number. It is next.	Draw a box around the number that ends the pattern. It is last.
④ 5 6	4 <u>5</u> 6	4 5 [6]

So, the number _____ is first. The number _____ is next.
The number _____ is last.

Check for Understanding

1. How do you know what number is first?

   _____

   _____

   _____

   _____

2. How do you know what number is next?

   _____

   _____

   _____

   _____

3. How do you know what number is last?

   _____

   _____

   _____

   _____

Identify Numbers to 30

Jason uses ● to show the number of goldfish he has.
How many goldfish does he have?

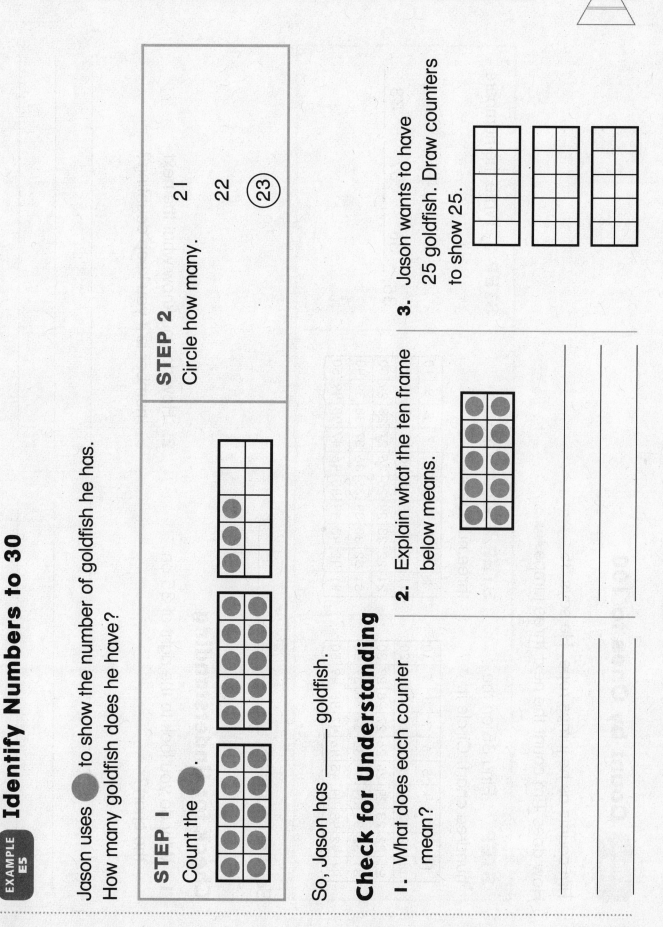

STEP 1
Count the ●.

STEP 2
Circle how many.

21

22

(23)

So, Jason has _____ goldfish.

Check for Understanding

1. What does each counter mean?

2. Explain what the ten frame below means.

3. Jason wants to have 25 goldfish. Draw counters to show 25.

_____

_____

EXAMPLE E6 Count by Ones to 100

Tim counts as he jumps rope. He says 35.
How does Tim count the next three jumps?

STEP I Find 35 on the hundred chart. Circle it.

1	2	3	4	5	6	7	8	9	10
11	12	13	14	15	16	17	18	19	20
21	22	23	24	25	26	27	28	29	30
31	32	33	34	(35)	36	37	38	39	40
41	42	43	44	45	46	47	48	49	50

STEP 2 Count forward three numbers.

1	2	3	4	5	6	7	8	9	10
11	12	13	14	15	16	17	18	19	20
21	22	23	24	25	26	27	28	29	30
31	32	33	34	(35)	36	37	38	39	40
41	42	43	44	45	46	47	48	49	50

STEP 3 Write the numbers.

35, __36__, __37__, __38__

So, Tim counts 35, _____, _____, _____.

Check for Understanding

1. Why do you look to the right of 35 on the chart?

_____

_____

2. How do you know what the next number is if you keep counting?

_____

_____

EXAMPLE E7

Count by Tens

Jan has 4 groups of 10 marbles. How many marbles does she have in all? Use the 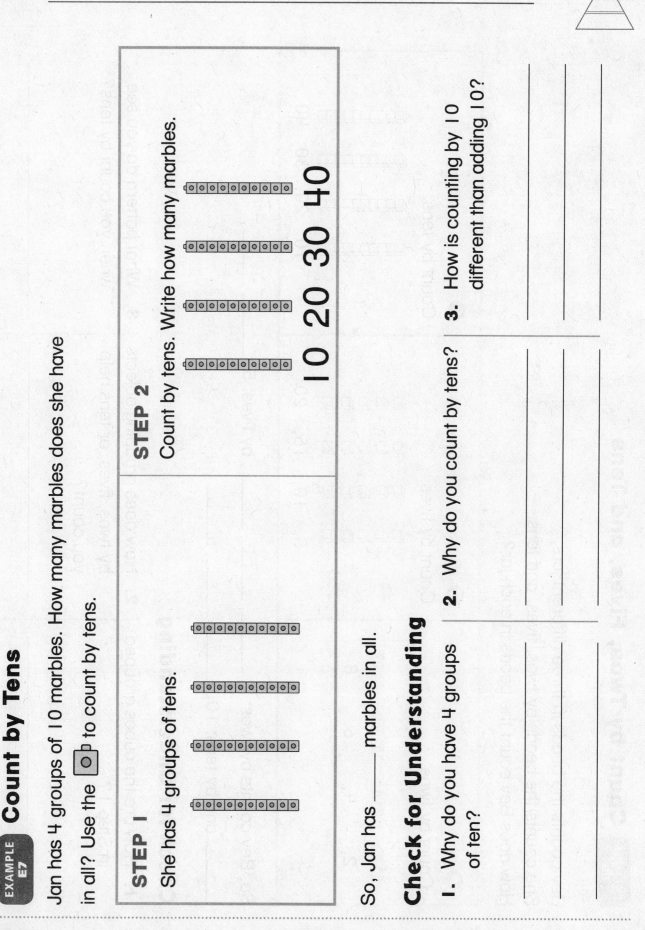 to count by tens.

STEP 1

She has 4 groups of tens.

STEP 2

Count by tens. Write how many marbles.

10 20 30 40

So, Jan has _____ marbles in all.

Check for Understanding

1. Why do you have 4 groups of ten?

    _____
    _____
    _____

2. Why do you count by tens?

    _____
    _____
    _____

3. How is counting by 10 different than adding 10?

    _____
    _____
    _____

EXAMPLE E8

Count by Twos, Fives, and Tens

Bev counts the beads in three different jars.
She counts the beads by twos, fives, and tens.
How does Bev count the beads in each jar?

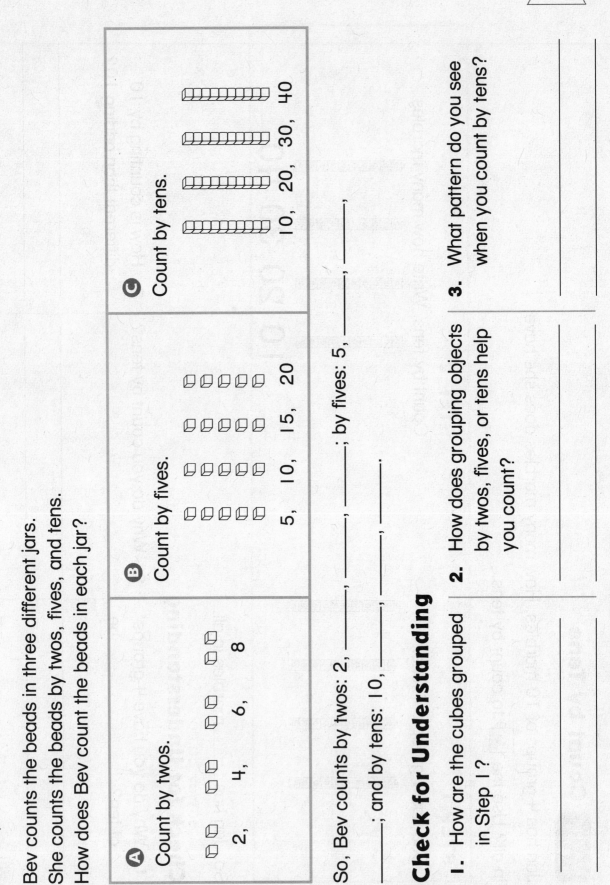

A Count by twos.

2, 4, 6, 8

B Count by fives.

5, 10, 15, 20

C Count by tens.

10, 20, 30, 40

So, Bev counts by twos: 2, ____, ____, ____; by fives: 5, ____, ____, ____; and by tens: 10, ____, ____, ____.

Check for Understanding

1. How are the cubes grouped in Step 1?

2. How does grouping objects by twos, fives, or tens help you count?

3. What pattern do you see when you count by tens?

EXAMPLE E9

Make a Model • Names for Numbers

Ed has 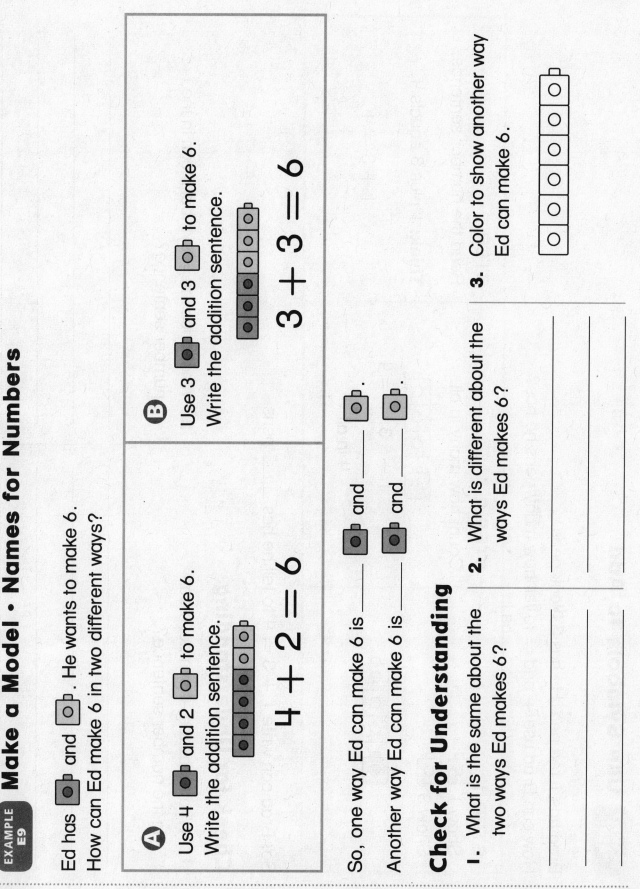 and 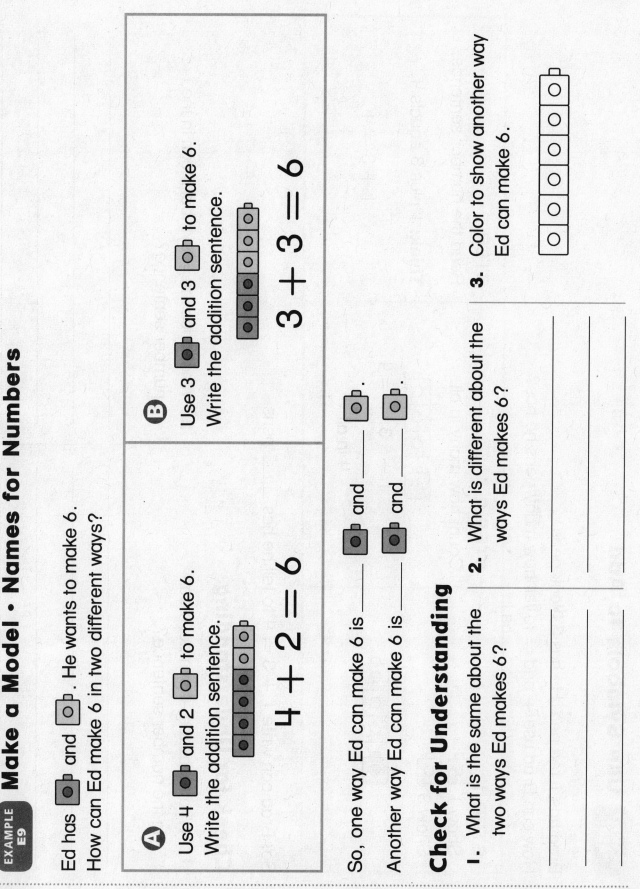. He wants to make 6.
How can Ed make 6 in two different ways?

A

Use 4 and 2 to make 6.
Write the addition sentence.

$$4 + 2 = 6$$

B

Use 3 and 3 to make 6.
Write the addition sentence.

$$3 + 3 = 6$$

So, one way Ed can make 6 is _____ and _____.

Another way Ed can make 6 is _____ and _____.

Check for Understanding

1. What is the same about the two ways Ed makes 6?

_____

_____

2. What is different about the ways Ed makes 6?

3. Color to show another way Ed can make 6.

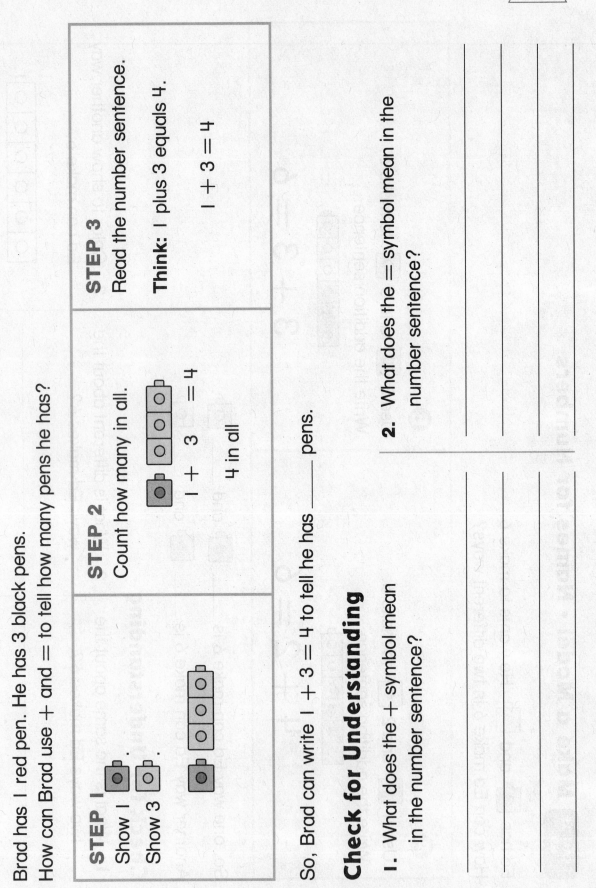

EXAMPLE E10

Use Symbols to Add

Brad has 1 red pen. He has 3 black pens.

How can Brad use + and = to tell how many pens he has?

STEP 1

Show 1.

Show 3.

STEP 2

Count how many in all.

1 + 3 = 4

4 in all

STEP 3

Read the number sentence.

Think: 1 plus 3 equals 4.

1 + 3 = 4

So, Brad can write 1 + 3 = 4 to tell he has _____ pens.

Check for Understanding

1. What does the + symbol mean in the number sentence?

2. What does the = symbol mean in the number sentence?

EXAMPLE E11

Algebra • Use Drawings to Represent Add to and Put Together Problems

T.J. sees 3 yellow dogs and 1 gray dog in the backyard.
How can T.J. show how many dogs there are?

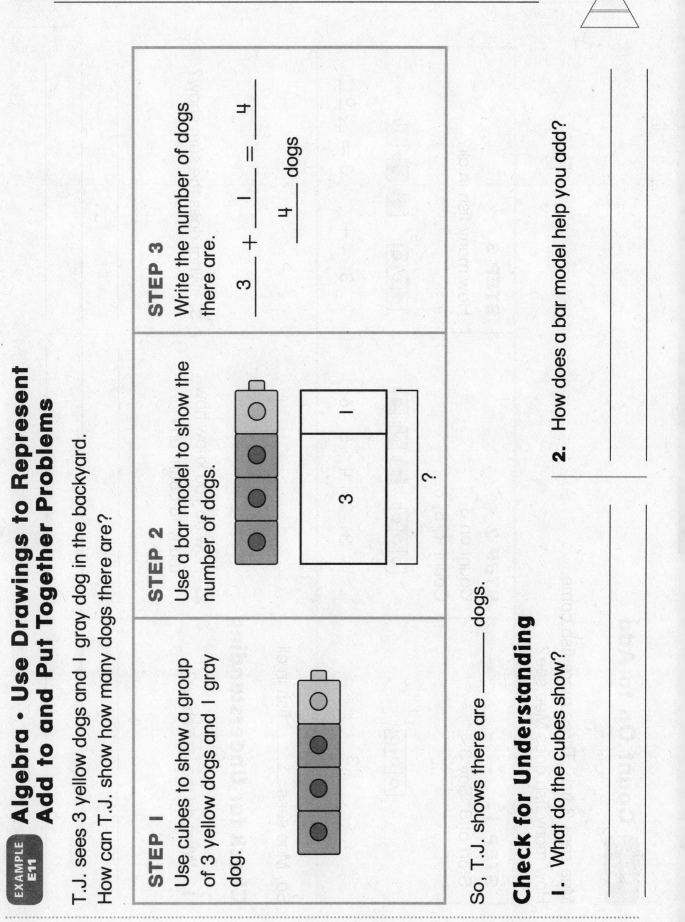

STEP 1

Use cubes to show a group of 3 yellow dogs and 1 gray dog.

STEP 2

Use a bar model to show the number of dogs.

3

1

?

STEP 3

Write the number of dogs there are.

3 + 1 = 4

_4_ dogs

So, T.J. shows there are _____ dogs.

Check for Understanding

1. What do the cubes show?

_____

2. How does a bar model help you add?

_____

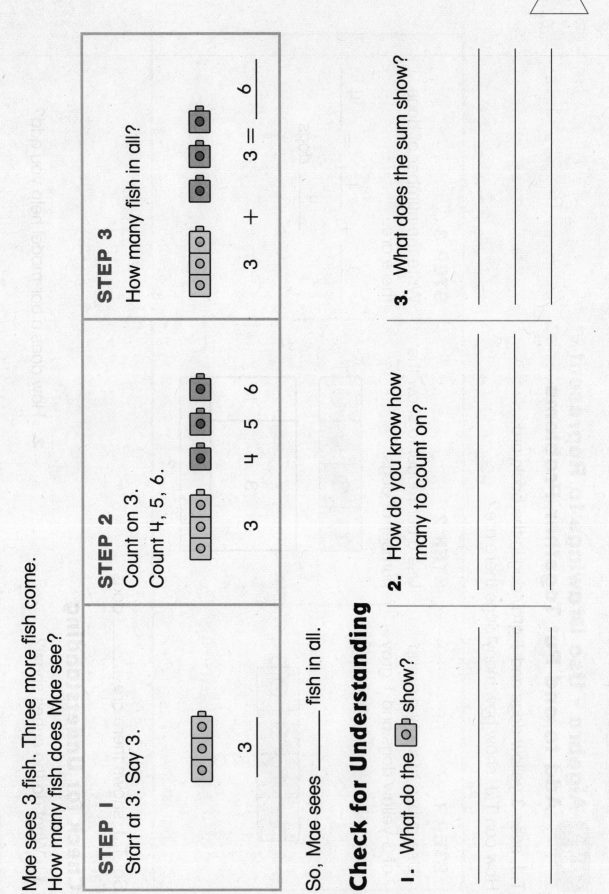

EXAMPLE E12

Count On to Add

Mae sees 3 fish. Three more fish come.
How many fish does Mae see?

STEP 1

Start at 3. Say 3.

3

STEP 2

Count on 3.
Count 4, 5, 6.

3   4 5 6

STEP 3

How many fish in all?

3   +   3 = __6__

So, Mae sees _____ fish in all.

Check for Understanding

1. What do the 🔲 show?

_____

2. How do you know how many to count on?

_____

3. What does the sum show?

_____

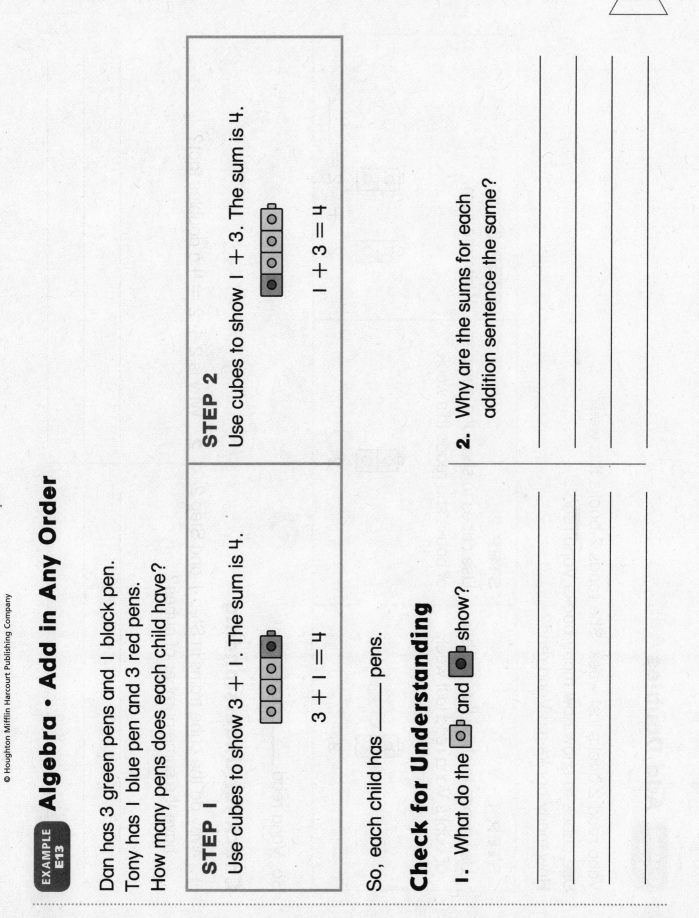

EXAMPLE E13

Algebra • Add in Any Order

Dan has 3 green pens and 1 black pen.
Tony has 1 blue pen and 3 red pens.
How many pens does each child have?

STEP 1

Use cubes to show 3 + 1. The sum is 4.

3 + 1 = 4

STEP 2

Use cubes to show 1 + 3. The sum is 4.

1 + 3 = 4

So, each child has ____ pens.

Check for Understanding

1. What do the ☐ and ☐ show?

_____

_____

_____

2. Why are the sums for each addition sentence the same?

_____

_____

_____

EXAMPLE E14 Add Doubles

Vana read 2 books last week. She reads 2 books this week.
Use cubes to show how many books Vana read.
How many books did Vana read?

STEP I

Use cubes to show the number of books Vana read last week.

2

STEP 2

Use cubes to show the number of books she reads this week.

2

STEP 3

Write the sum.

2 + 2 = __4__

So, Vana read _____ books.

Check for Understanding

I. Why do the cube trains in Step I and Step 2 have the same number of cubes?

_____

_____

_____

2. Why is 2 + 2 = 4 a doubles fact?

_____

_____

_____

EXAMPLE E15

Doubles and Doubles Plus One

Tom has 2 books. Mari has 3 books.
How many books do they have?

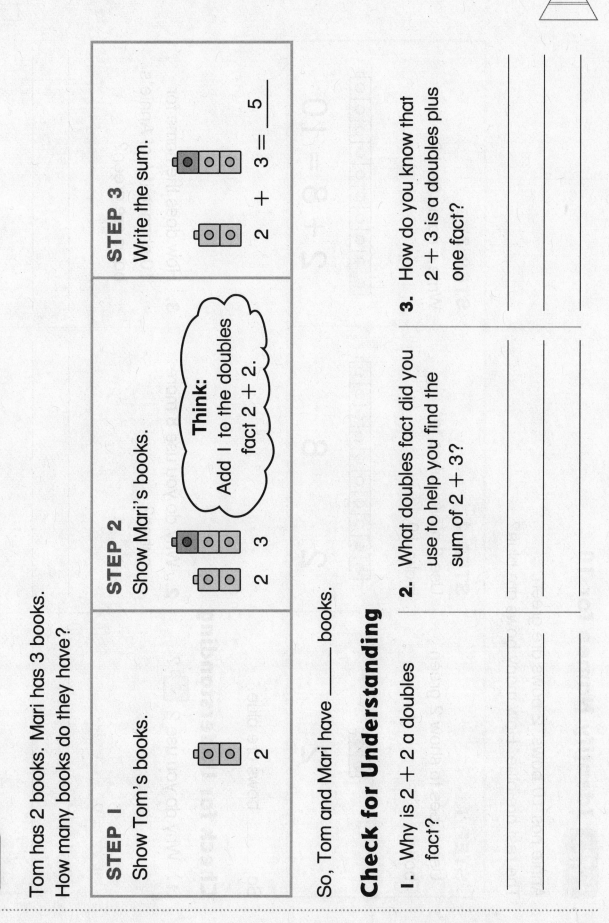

STEP 1

Show Tom's books.

2

STEP 2

Show Mari's books.

2   3

Think:
Add 1 to the doubles fact 2 + 2.

STEP 3

Write the sum.

2 + 3 = _5_

So, Tom and Mari have _____ books.

Check for Understanding

1. Why is 2 + 2 a doubles fact?

2. What doubles fact did you use to help you find the sum of 2 + 3?

3. How do you know that 2 + 3 is a doubles plus one fact?

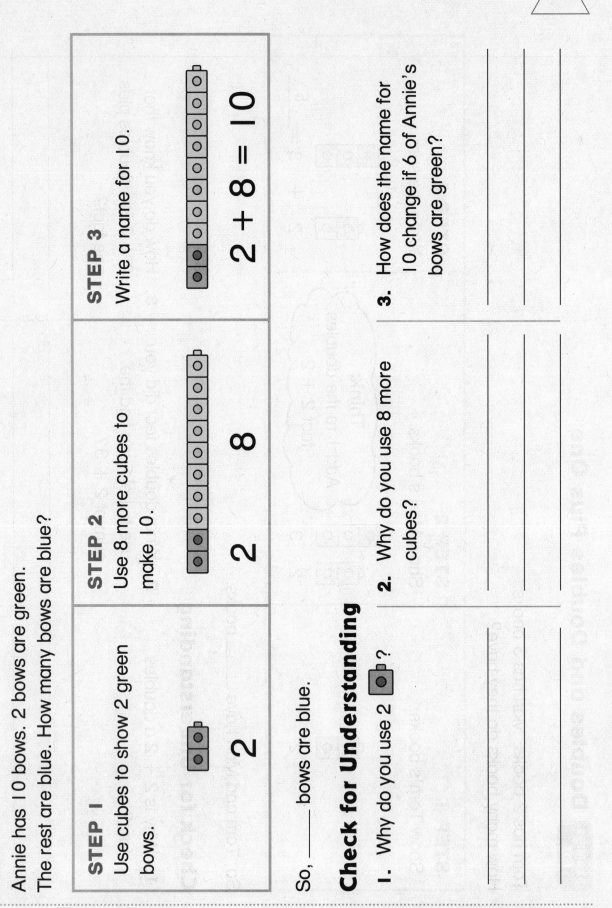

EXAMPLE E16

Identify Names for 10

Annie has 10 bows. 2 bows are green.
The rest are blue. How many bows are blue?

STEP 1

Use cubes to show 2 green bows.

2

STEP 2

Use 8 more cubes to make 10.

2   8

STEP 3

Write a name for 10.

$2 + 8 = 10$

So, _____ bows are blue.

Check for Understanding

1. Why do you use 2 ⬡ ?
_____
_____
_____

2. Why do you use 8 more cubes?
_____
_____

3. How does the name for 10 change if 6 of Annie's bows are green?
_____
_____
_____

EXAMPLE E17

Make a Ten

Luis has 7 marbles. Kim has 4 marbles.
How many marbles do Luis and Kim have?

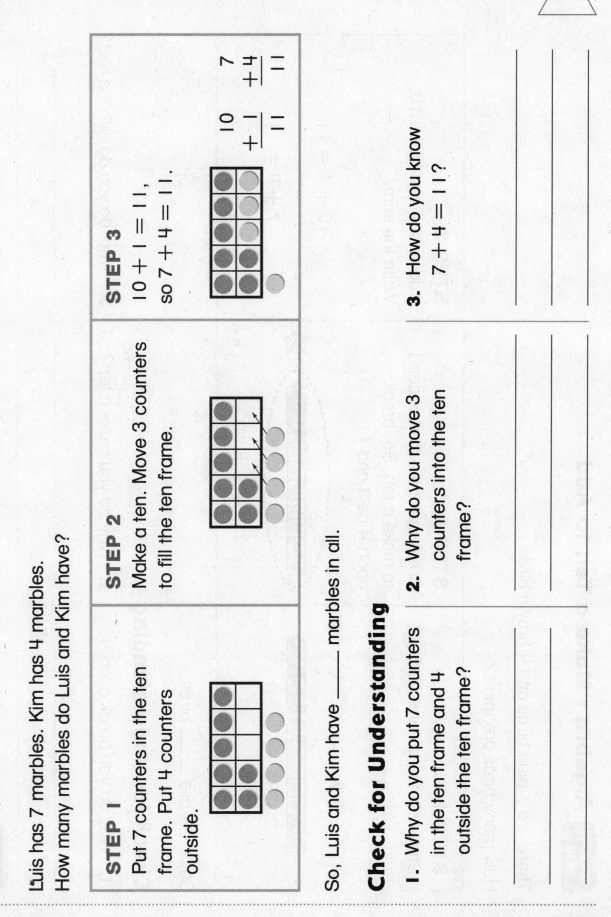

STEP 1

Put 7 counters in the ten frame. Put 4 counters outside.

STEP 2

Make a ten. Move 3 counters to fill the ten frame.

STEP 3

$10 + 1 = 11$,
so $7 + 4 = 11$.

$$\begin{array}{r} 10 \\ + 1 \\ \hline 11 \end{array} \qquad \begin{array}{r} 7 \\ + 4 \\ \hline 11 \end{array}$$

So, Luis and Kim have _____ marbles in all.

Check for Understanding

1. Why do you put 7 counters in the ten frame and 4 outside the ten frame?

_____

_____

2. Why do you move 3 counters into the ten frame?

_____

_____

3. How do you know $7 + 4 = 11$?

_____

_____

EXAMPLE E18

Algebra • Make a Ten to Add

There are 7 blue birds and 4 brown birds.

How many birds are there?

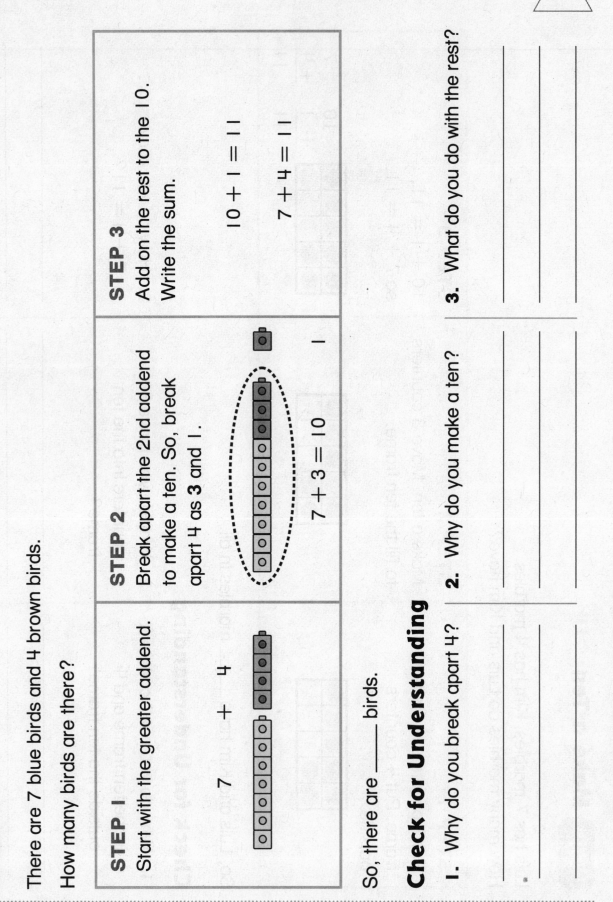

STEP 1

Start with the greater addend.

7 + 4

STEP 2

Break apart the 2nd addend to make a ten. So, break apart **4** as **3** and **1**.

7 + 3 = 10

STEP 3

Add on the rest to the 10. Write the sum.

10 + 1 = 11

7 + 4 = 11

So, there are _____ birds.

Check for Understanding

1. Why do you break apart 4?

_____

_____

2. Why do you make a ten?

_____

_____

3. What do you do with the rest?

_____

_____

EXAMPLE E19

Addition Patterns

There is 1 frog on a log.
1 more frog hops on the log.
How many frogs are on the log now?

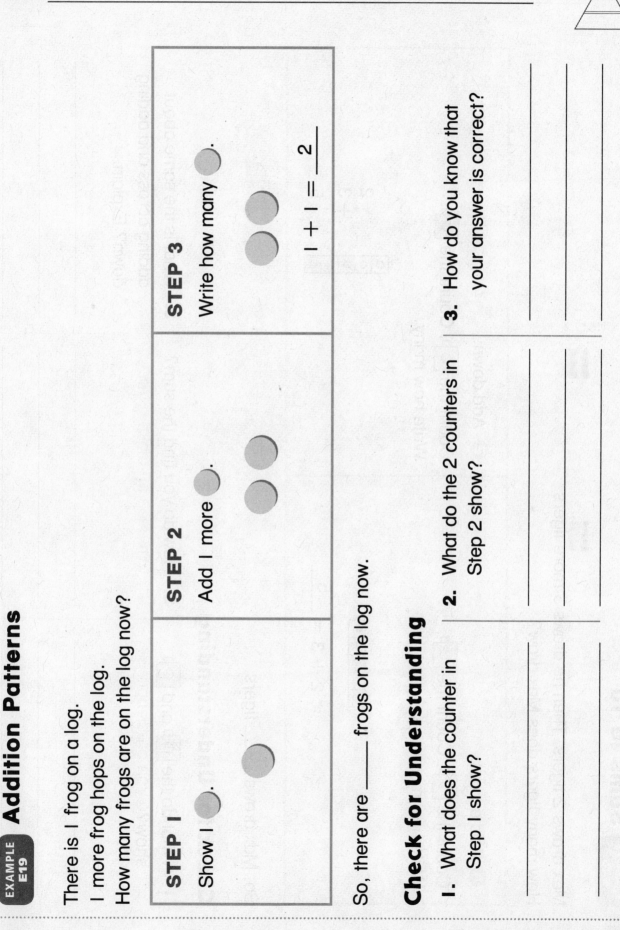

STEP 1
Show 1 ●.

STEP 2
Add 1 more ●.

STEP 3
Write how many ●.

1 + 1 = ___2___

So, there are _____ frogs on the log now.

Check for Understanding

1. What does the counter in Step 1 show?

_____

_____

2. What do the 2 counters in Step 2 show?

_____

_____

3. How do you know that your answer is correct?

_____

_____

_____

EXAMPLE E20 Sums to 10

Max draws 2 tigers. Then he draws 3 more tigers.
How many tigers does Max draw?

A Add across.

Count the 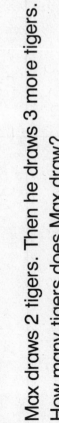. Count the 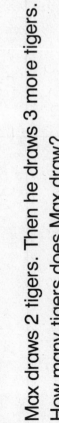.
Write how many.

$2 + 3 = \underline{\ \ 5\ \ }$

B Add down.

Count the 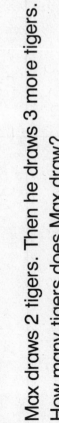. Count the 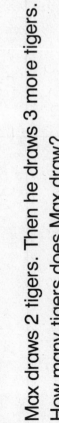.
Write how many.

$$\begin{array}{r} 2 \\ + 3 \\ \hline 5 \end{array}$$

So, Max draws _____ tigers.

Check for Understanding

1. What do the 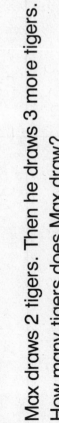 and 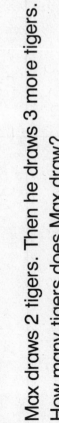 show?

2. How do you find the sum?

3. What is the same about adding across and adding down? Explain.

EXAMPLE E21 **Sums to 12**

Ben has 4 blue boats and 5 red boats.
How many boats does Ben have?

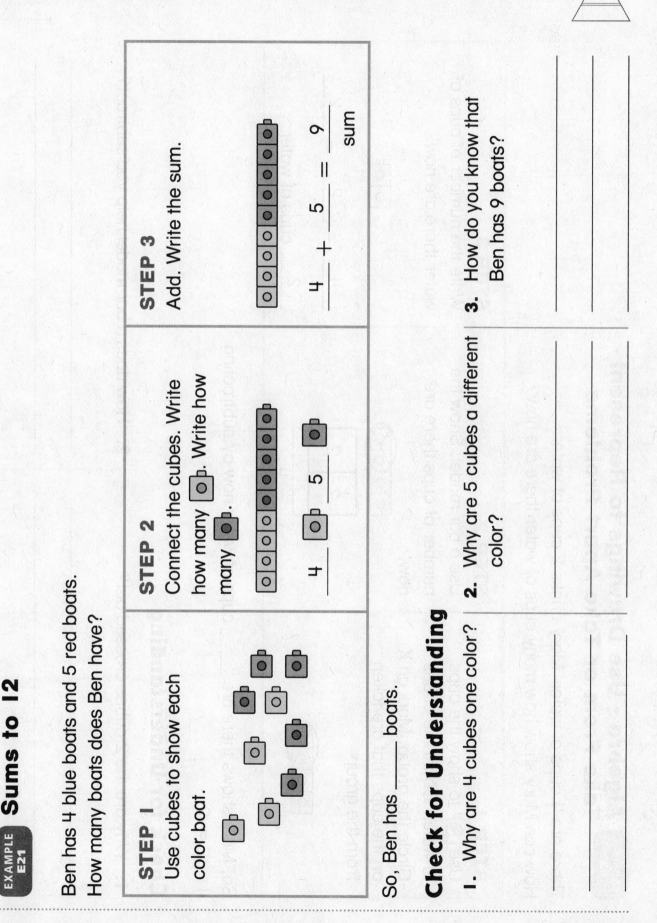

STEP 1
Use cubes to show each color boat.

STEP 2
Connect the cubes. Write how many ▣. Write how many ▣.

4
5

STEP 3
Add. Write the sum.

4
+ 5
= 9
sum

So, Ben has ____ boats.

Check for Understanding

1. Why are 4 cubes one color?

2. Why are 5 cubes a different color?

3. How do you know that Ben has 9 boats?

EXAMPLE E22 · Algebra · Use Drawings to Represent Take From or Take Apart Problems

There are 4 cups of water. Mary drinks 2 cups of water.
How can Mary show how many cups of water there are now?

STEP 1

Use 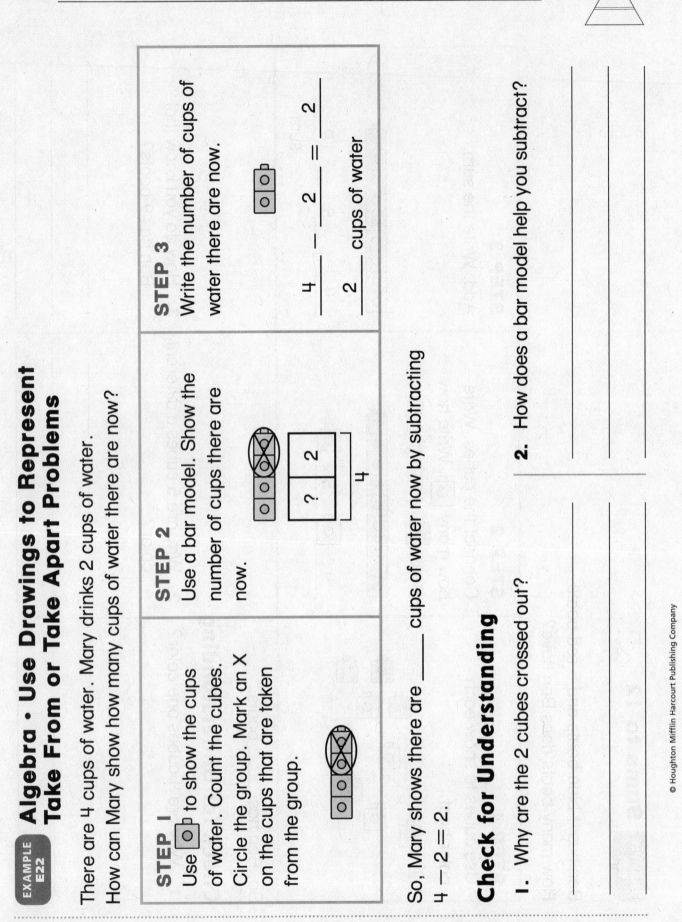 to show the cups of water. Count the cubes. Circle the group. Mark an X on the cups that are taken from the group.

STEP 2

Use a bar model. Show the number of cups there are now.

?	2

4

STEP 3

Write the number of cups of water there are now.

$$4$$
$$-\ 2$$
$$2 - 2 = 2$$
$$\underline{\hspace{1cm}2\hspace{1cm}}\ \text{cups of water}$$

So, Mary shows there are _____ cups of water now by subtracting
4 − 2 = 2.

Check for Understanding

1. Why are the 2 cubes crossed out?

_____

_____

2. How does a bar model help you subtract?

_____

_____

_____

E22

Example E22

© Houghton Mifflin Harcourt Publishing Company

EXAMPLE E23

Algebra • Use Drawings to Represent Compare Problems

Chaz has 4 flowers. Sheri has 3 flowers.
How many more flowers does Chaz have than Sheri?

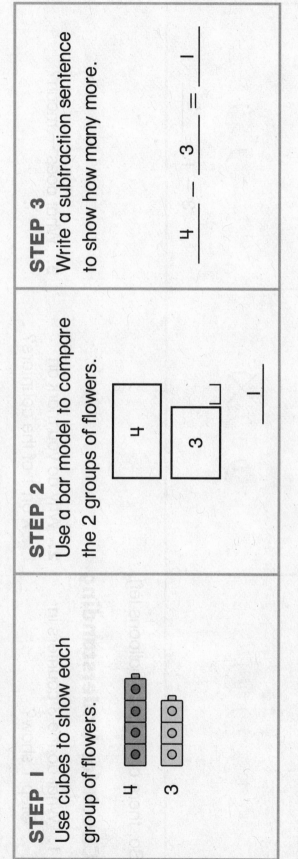

STEP 1

Use cubes to show each group of flowers.

4

3

STEP 2

Use a bar model to compare the 2 groups of flowers.

4

3

STEP 3

Write a subtraction sentence to show how many more.

$$4 - 3 = 1$$

So, Chaz has _____ more flower than Sheri.

Check for Understanding

1. How can a bar model be used to compare 4 and 3?

   _____

2. How do you know Chaz has 1 more flower than Sheri?

   _____

EXAMPLE E24 Subtraction Patterns

There are 3 balloons.
1 balloon flies away.
How many balloons are left?

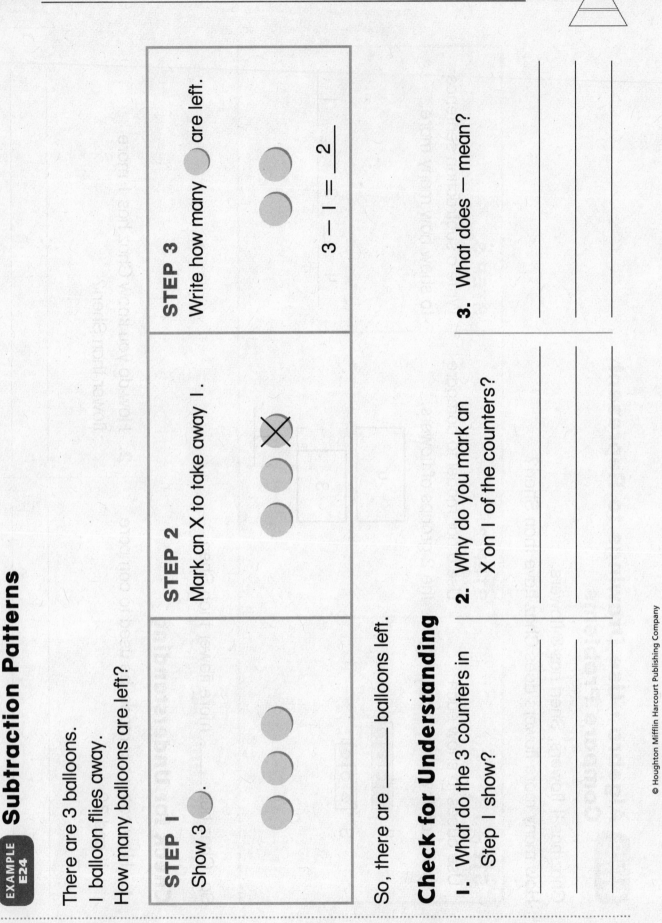

STEP 1
Show 3.

STEP 2
Mark an X to take away 1.

STEP 3
Write how many ◯ are left.

3 – 1 = __2__

So, there are _____ balloons left.

Check for Understanding

1. What do the 3 counters in Step 1 show?

_____

_____

2. Why do you mark an X on 1 of the counters?

_____

_____

3. What does – mean?

_____

_____

EXAMPLE E25

Differences to 10

There are 5 birds in a tree. Then 2 birds fly away.
How many birds are in the tree now?

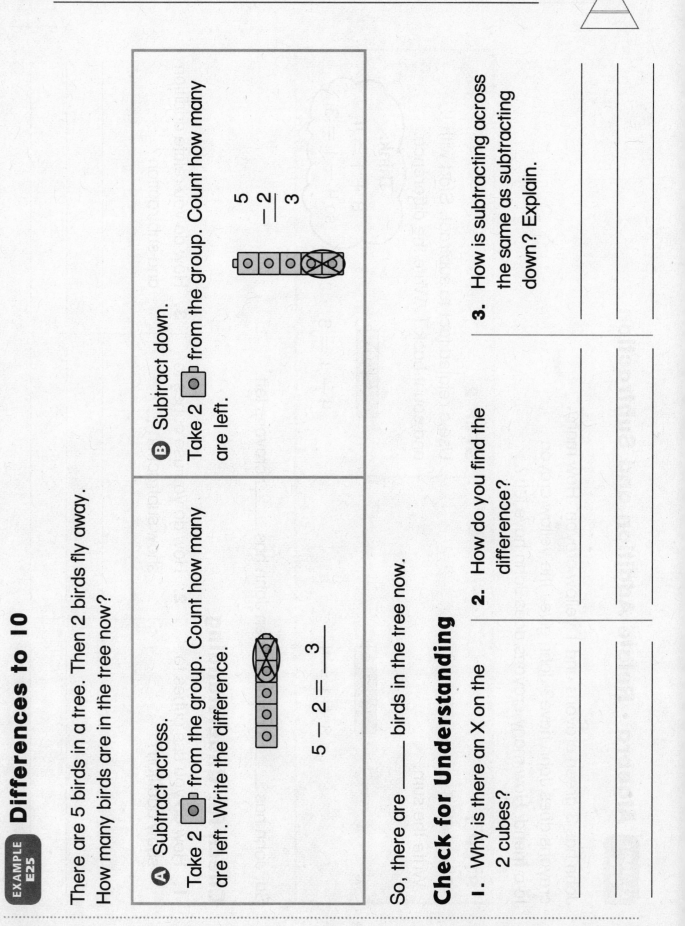

A Subtract across.

Take 2 ○ from the group. Count how many
are left. Write the difference.

$$5 - 2 = \underline{}\,3$$

B Subtract down.

Take 2 ○ from the group. Count how many
are left.

$$\begin{array}{r} 5 \\ -\,2 \\ \hline 3 \end{array}$$

So, there are _____ birds in the tree now.

Check for Understanding

1. Why is there an X on the
2 cubes?

_____

_____

2. How do you find the
difference?

_____

_____

3. How is subtracting across
the same as subtracting
down? Explain.

_____

_____

_____

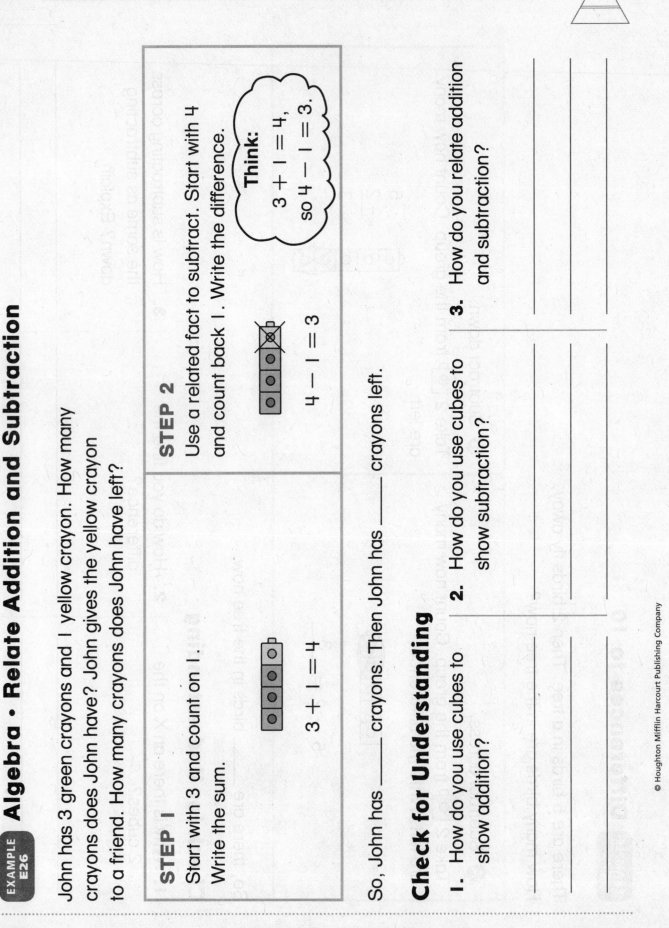

EXAMPLE E26

Algebra • Relate Addition and Subtraction

John has 3 green crayons and 1 yellow crayon. How many crayons does John have? John gives the yellow crayon to a friend. How many crayons does John have left?

STEP 1

Start with 3 and count on 1. Write the sum. _____

$3 + 1 = 4$

STEP 2

Use a related fact to subtract. Start with 4 and count back 1. Write the difference.

$4 - 1 = 3$

Think:

$3 + 1 = 4$,
so $4 - 1 = 3$.

So, John has _____ crayons. Then John has _____ crayons left.

Check for Understanding

1. How do you use cubes to show addition?

_____

_____

2. How do you use cubes to show subtraction?

_____

_____

3. How do you relate addition and subtraction?

_____

_____

EXAMPLE E27

Count Back

There are 5 bugs on a leaf. Then 2 bugs crawl away.
How many bugs are left on the leaf?

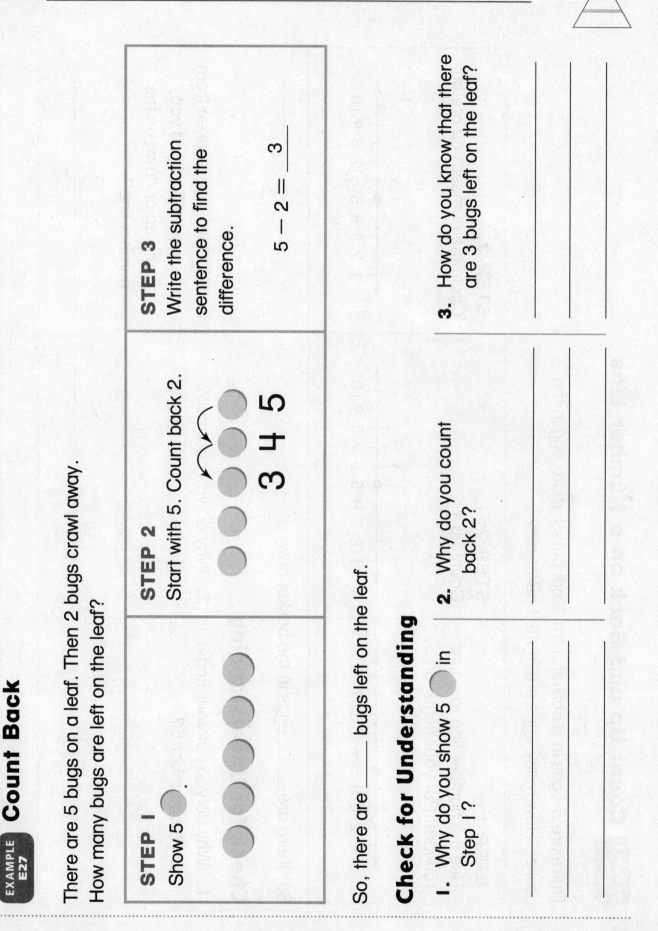

STEP 1
Show 5.

STEP 2
Start with 5. Count back 2.

3 4 5

STEP 3
Write the subtraction sentence to find the difference.

5 − 2 = __3__

So, there are _____ bugs left on the leaf.

Check for Understanding

1. Why do you show 5 in Step 1?

_____

2. Why do you count back 2?

_____

3. How do you know that there are 3 bugs left on the leaf?

_____

EXAMPLE E28   Count Up and Back on a Number Line

There are 5 eggs in a basket. Mrs. Pool puts 1 more egg in the basket. How many eggs are in the basket now?

STEP 1
Use the number line to count forward. Put your finger on 5.

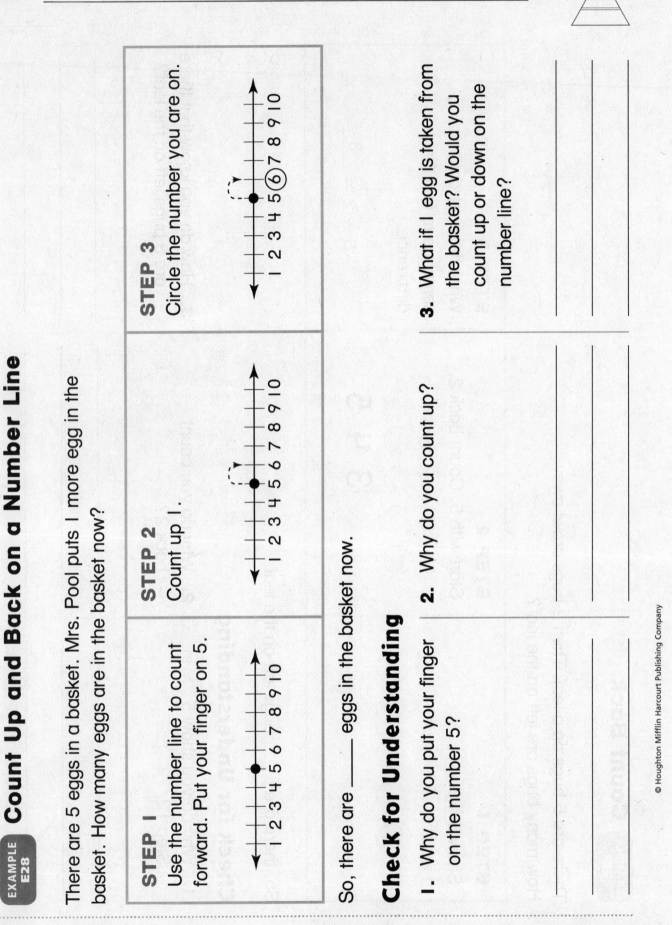

STEP 2
Count up 1.

STEP 3
Circle the number you are on.

So, there are _____ eggs in the basket now.

Check for Understanding

1. Why do you put your finger on the number 5?

_____

_____

2. Why do you count up?

_____

_____

3. What if 1 egg is taken from the basket? Would you count up or down on the number line?

_____

_____

EXAMPLE E29 **Use Ten to Subtract**

There are 11 marbles in a bag.
4 marbles roll out of the bag.
How many marbles are left in the bag?

STEP 1

Start with 11 [🔲].

Subtract one to get to 10.

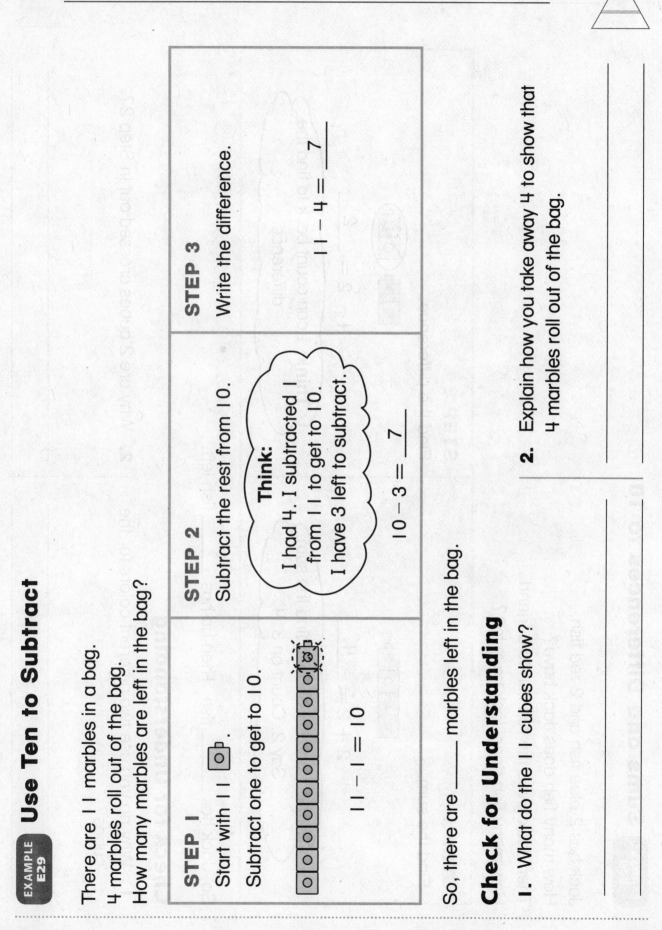

11 − 1 = 10

STEP 2

Subtract the rest from 10.

Think:
I had 4. I subtracted 1
from 11 to get to 10.
I have 3 left to subtract.

10 − 3 = ___7___

STEP 3

Write the difference.

11 − 4 = ___7___

So, there are _____ marbles left in the bag.

Check for Understanding

1. What do the 11 cubes show?

_____

2. Explain how you take away 4 to show that
   4 marbles roll out of the bag.

_____

Sums and Differences to 10

Jack has 2 blue fish and 2 red fish.
How many fish does Jack have?
Then Jack gives the red fish to a friend.
How many fish does Jack have left?

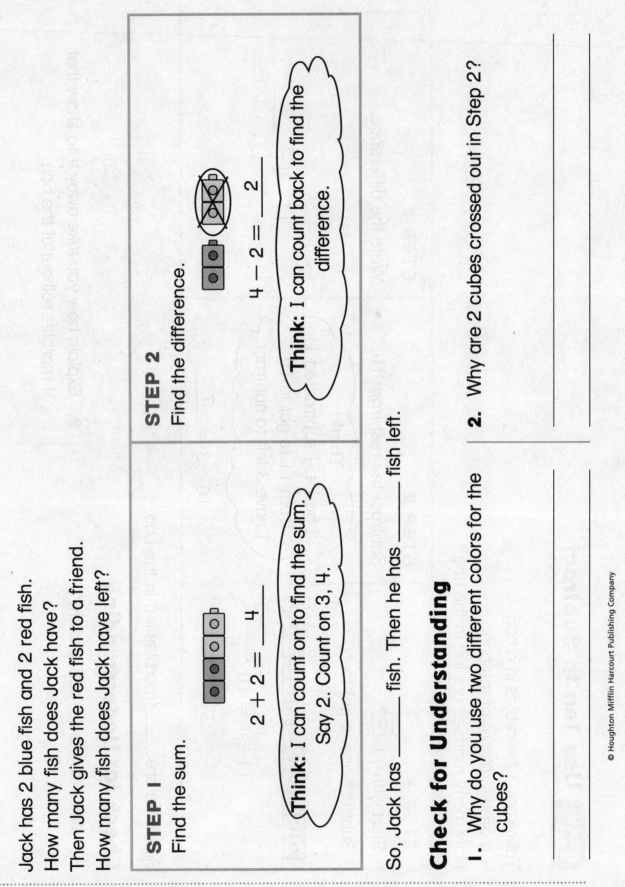

STEP 1
Find the sum.

$2 + 2 = \underline{}4$

Think: I can count on to find the sum.
Say 2. Count on 3, 4.

STEP 2
Find the difference.

$4 - 2 = \underline{}2$

Think: I can count back to find the difference.

So, Jack has _____ fish. Then he has _____ fish left.

Check for Understanding

1. Why do you use two different colors for the cubes?

_____

_____

2. Why are 2 cubes crossed out in Step 2?

_____

_____

EXAMPLE E31

Explore Tens

There are 2 bags of apples. Each bag has 10 apples. How many apples are there? Use 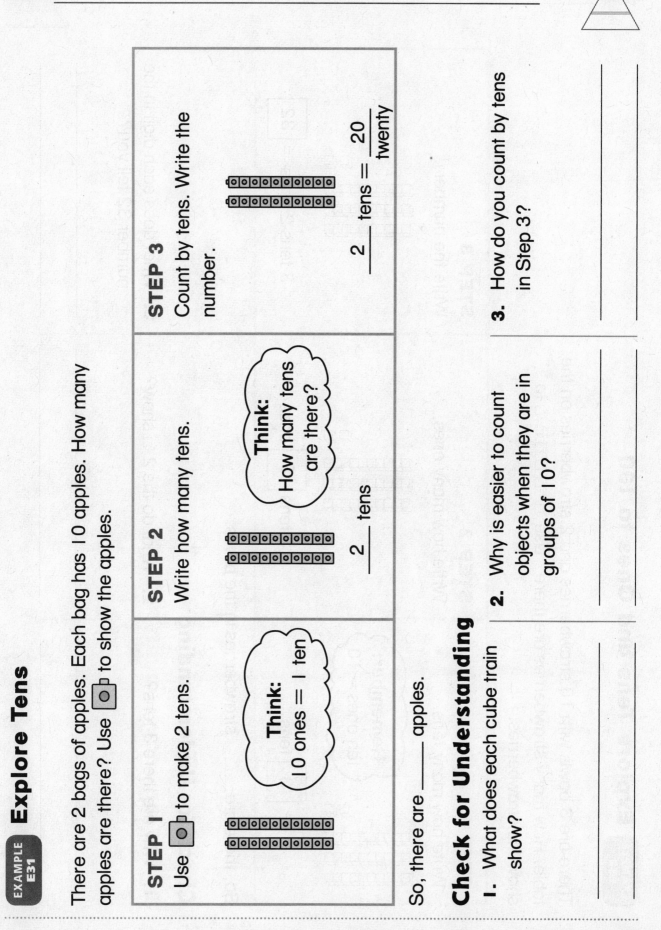 to show the apples.

STEP 1

Use ◉ to make 2 tens.

Think:
10 ones = 1 ten

STEP 2

Write how many tens.

Think:
How many tens are there?

_2_ tens

STEP 3

Count by tens. Write the number.

_2_ tens = _20_
twenty

So, there are _____ apples.

Check for Understanding

1. What does each cube train show?

2. Why is easier to count objects when they are in groups of 10?

3. How do you count by tens in Step 3?

Explore Tens and Ones to 100

There are 3 bowls with 10 strawberries and 2 strawberries on the table. How many strawberries are there? Use ▭▭▭▭▭▭▭▭▭▭ ▯ to show the strawberries.

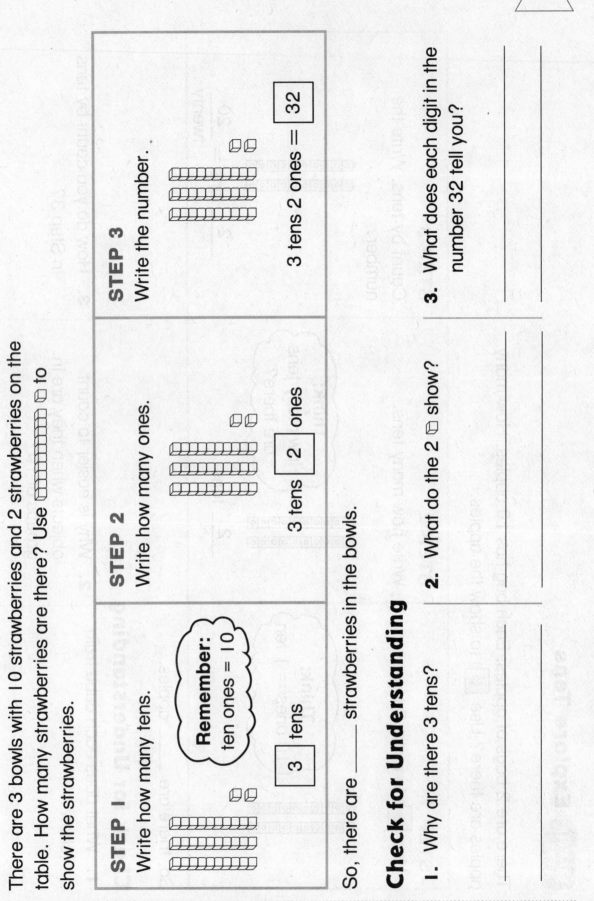

STEP 1
Write how many tens.

> **Remember:** ten ones = 10

[3] tens

STEP 2
Write how many ones.

3 tens [2] ones

STEP 3
Write the number.

3 tens 2 ones = [32]

So, there are _____ strawberries in the bowls.

Check for Understanding

1. Why are there 3 tens?

_____

_____

2. What do the 2 ▯ show?

_____

_____

3. What does each digit in the number 32 tell you?

_____

_____

Name _____

EXAMPLE E33 Model Tens and Ones to 100

Sam has 3 packs of pencils. Each pack has 10 pencils.
Kim gives him 4 more pencils.
How many pencils does Sam have now?

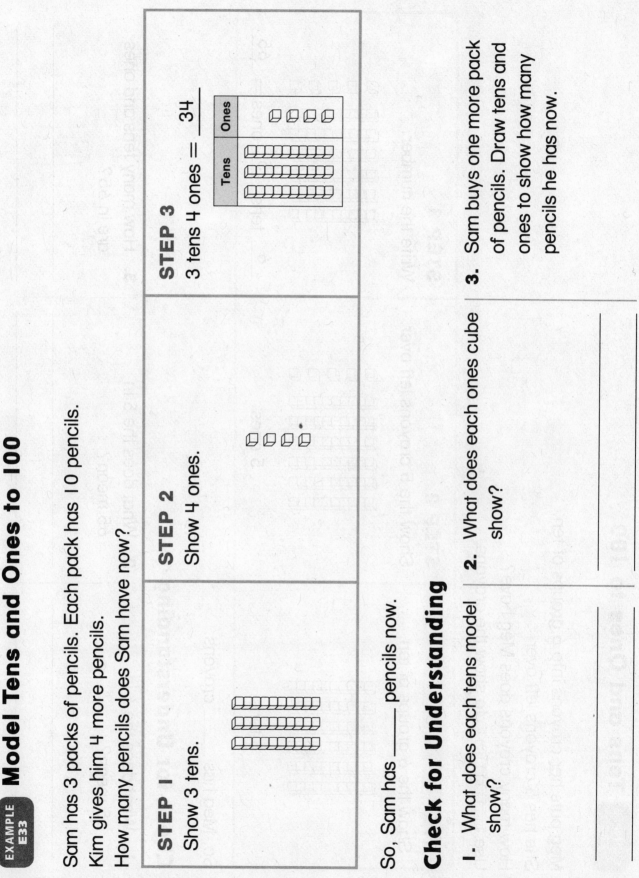

STEP 1
Show 3 tens.

STEP 2
Show 4 ones.

STEP 3
3 tens 4 ones = ___34___

Tens	Ones

So, Sam has _____ pencils now.

Check for Understanding

1. What does each tens model show?

_____

2. What does each ones cube show?

_____

3. Sam buys one more pack of pencils. Draw tens and ones to show how many pencils he has now.

EXAMPLE E34 Tens and Ones to 100

Meg puts her crayons into 6 groups of ten.
She has 5 crayons left over.
How many crayons does Meg have?
Use 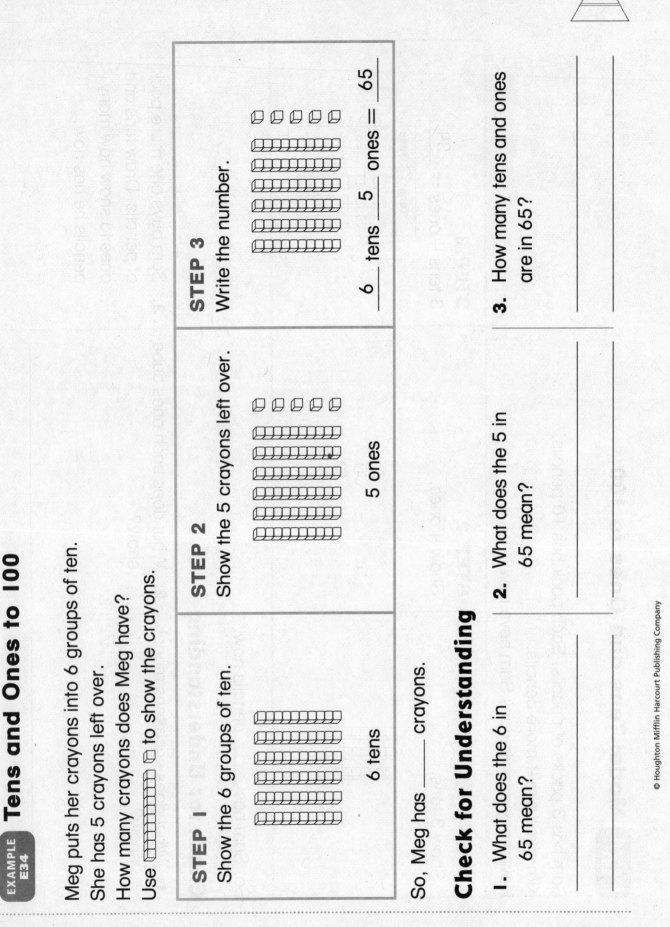 to show the crayons.

STEP 1	STEP 2	STEP 3
Show the 6 groups of ten.	Show the 5 crayons left over.	Write the number.
6 tens	5 ones	6 tens 5 ones = 65

So, Meg has _____ crayons.

Check for Understanding

1. What does the 6 in 65 mean?

_____

2. What does the 5 in 65 mean?

_____

3. How many tens and ones are in 65?

_____

Name _____

EXAMPLE E35

Understand Place Value

After a party, Joe has 2 packs of 10 balloons and 3 more balloons left over. How many balloons are left over?

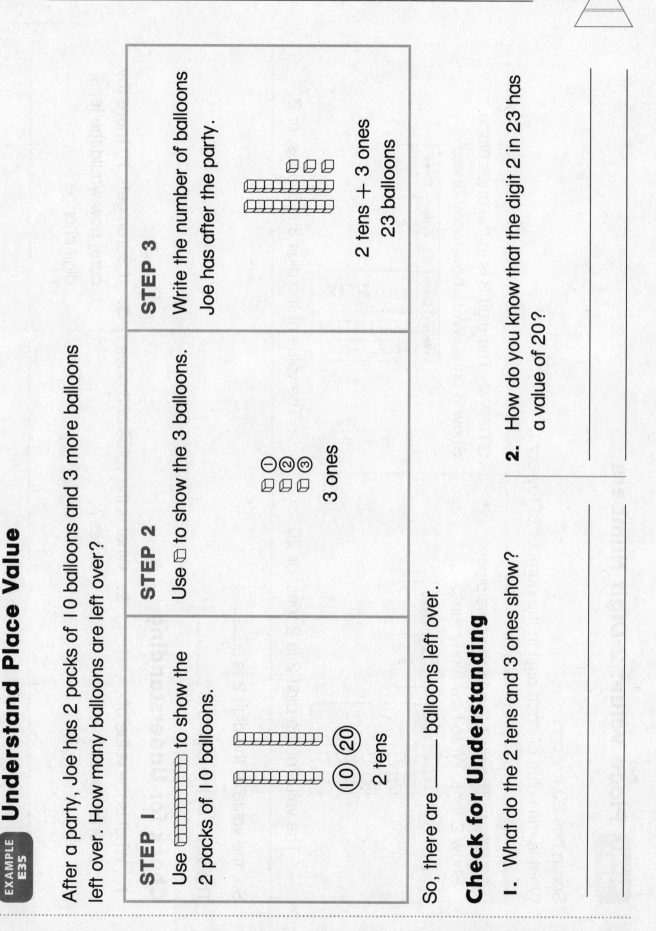

STEP 1

Use [⬚⬚⬚⬚⬚⬚⬚⬚⬚⬚] to show the 2 packs of 10 balloons.

⑩ ⑳

2 tens

STEP 2

Use ▢ to show the 3 balloons.

① ② ③

3 ones

STEP 3

Write the number of balloons Joe has after the party.

2 tens + 3 ones

23 balloons

So, there are _____ balloons left over.

Check for Understanding

1. What do the 2 tens and 3 ones show?

_____

2. How do you know that the digit 2 in 23 has a value of 20?

_____

Place Value: 2-Digit Numbers

EXAMPLE E36

Soren has 23 toy cars.

What is the value of each digit in the number of toy cars?

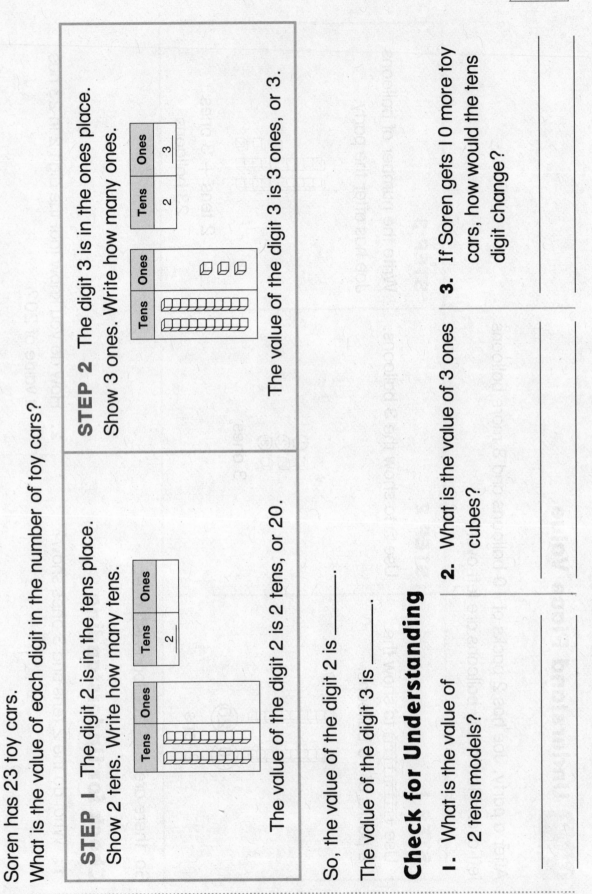

STEP 1 The digit 2 is in the tens place.
Show 2 tens. Write how many tens.

Tens	Ones
2	

The value of the digit 2 is 2 tens, or 20.

STEP 2 The digit 3 is in the ones place.
Show 3 ones. Write how many ones.

Tens	Ones
2	3

The value of the digit 3 is 3 ones, or 3.

So, the value of the digit 2 is _____.

The value of the digit 3 is _____.

Check for Understanding

1. What is the value of
   2 tens models?

   _____

2. What is the value of 3 ones
   cubes?

   _____

3. If Soren gets 10 more toy
   cars, how would the tens
   digit change?

   _____

EXAMPLE E37

Different Ways to Write Numbers

Brad finds 25 shells at the beach.

How can Brad write the number 25 in different ways?

STEP 1

Write how many tens.
Write how many ones.

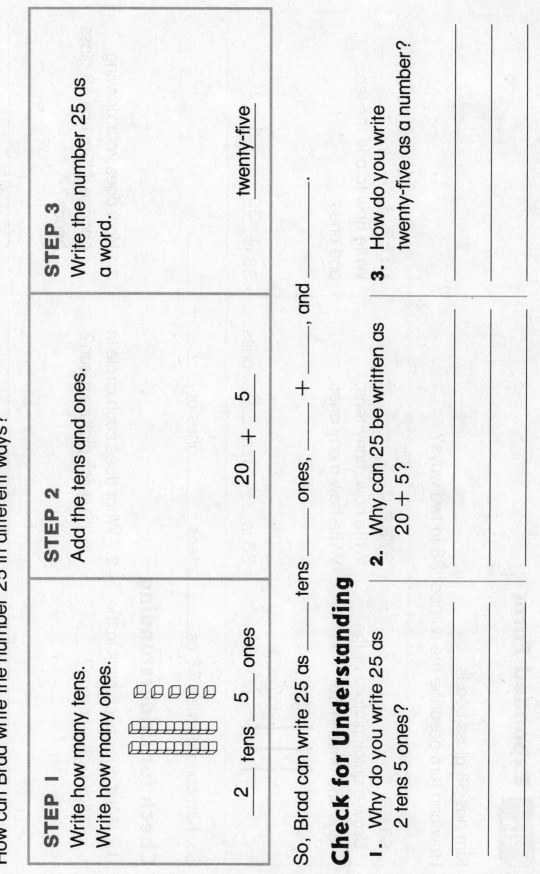

__2__ tens __5__ ones

STEP 2

Add the tens and ones.

__20__ + __5__

STEP 3

Write the number 25 as a word.

__twenty-five__

So, Brad can write 25 as ____ tens ____ ones, ____ + ____, and ____.

Check for Understanding

1. Why do you write 25 as 2 tens 5 ones?

_____

_____

_____

2. Why can 25 be written as 20 + 5?

_____

_____

_____

3. How do you write twenty-five as a number?

_____

_____

_____

EXAMPLE E38

Expanded Form

Kim has 38 glass beads.
How can Kim describe the number 38 in two ways?

STEP 1

Draw a quick picture of the tens and ones in 38.

STEP 2

Write how many tens.
Write how many ones.

38 is __3__ tens __8__ ones.

STEP 3

Write how to add the tens and ones.

38 is __30__ + __8__.

So, Kim can describe 38 as _____ tens _____ ones or _____ + _____.

Check for Understanding

1. What does each stick in the quick picture mean?

_____

_____

_____

2. What does each circle in the quick picture mean?

_____

_____

_____

3. How does your drawing change if Kim has 68 glass beads?

_____

_____

_____

Name _____

EXAMPLE E39

10 Less, 10 More

Jeff rides his bike for 23 minutes. Meg rides her bike 10 minutes less. John rides his bike 10 minutes more. For how many minutes do Meg and John ride their bikes?

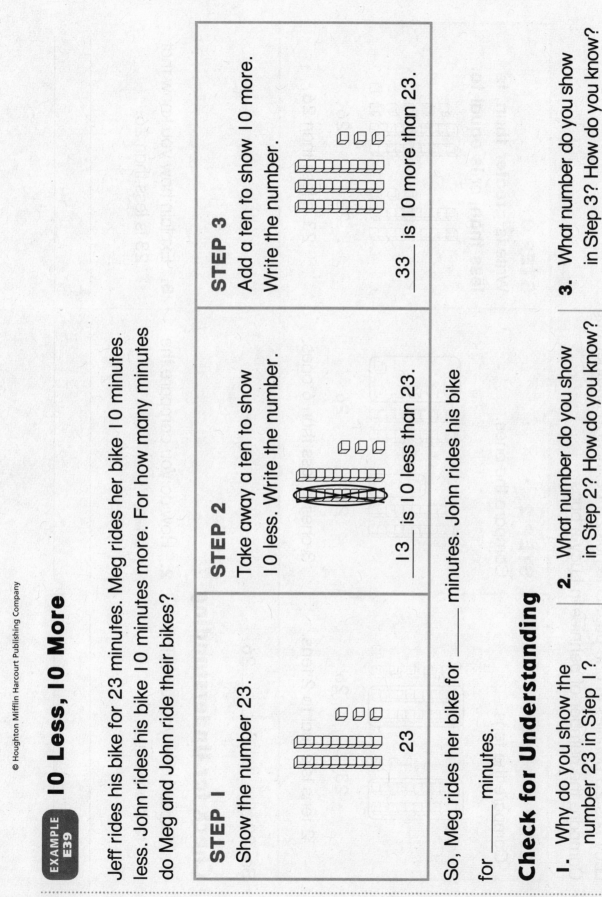

STEP 1

Show the number 23.

23

STEP 2

Take away a ten to show 10 less. Write the number.

13 is 10 less than 23.

STEP 3

Add a ten to show 10 more. Write the number.

33 is 10 more than 23.

So, Meg rides her bike for _____ minutes. John rides his bike

for _____ minutes.

Check for Understanding

1. Why do you show the number 23 in Step 1?

   _____

2. What number do you show in Step 2? How do you know?

   _____

3. What number do you show in Step 3? How do you know?

   _____

EXAMPLE E40 Compare 2-Digit Numbers

Lucy has 23 pennies in one bag. She has 26 pennies in another bag.
Compare the number of pennies in Lucy's bags.

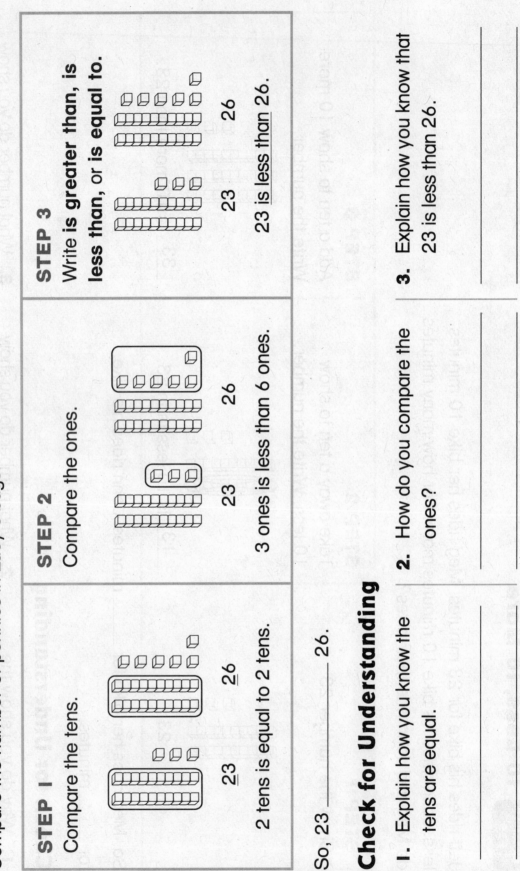

STEP 1

Compare the tens.

23   <u>26</u>

2 tens is equal to 2 tens.

STEP 2

Compare the ones.

23   26

3 ones is less than 6 ones.

STEP 3

Write **is greater than**, **is less than**, or **is equal to.**

23   26

23 is <u>less than</u> 26.

So, 23 _____ 26.

Check for Understanding

1. Explain how you know the tens are equal.

_____

_____

2. How do you compare the ones?

_____

_____

3. Explain how you know that 23 is less than 26.

_____

_____

_____

EXAMPLE E41

Compare Numbers

Jane counts 29 people at the park one day. She counts 22 people at the park the next day. How can she compare the numbers?

Think:
> means is greater than.
< means is less than.

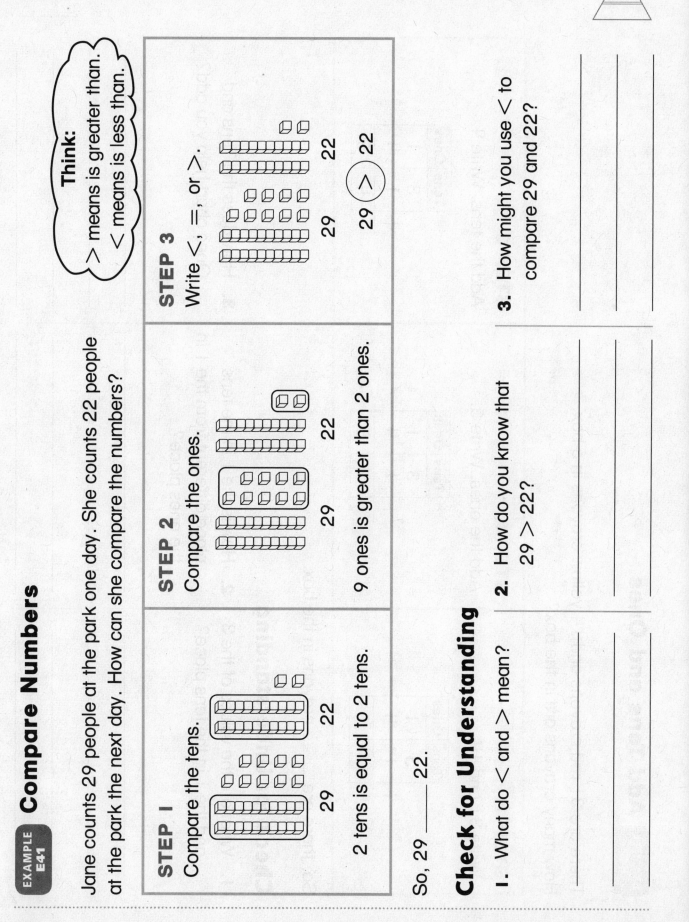

STEP I

Compare the tens.

29

22

2 tens is equal to 2 tens.

STEP 2

Compare the ones.

29

22

9 ones is greater than 2 ones.

STEP 3

Write <, =, or >.

29

22

29 (>) 22

So, 29 ____ 22.

Check for Understanding

1. What do < and > mean?

_____

_____

2. How do you know that 29 > 22?

_____

_____

3. How might you use < to compare 29 and 22?

_____

_____

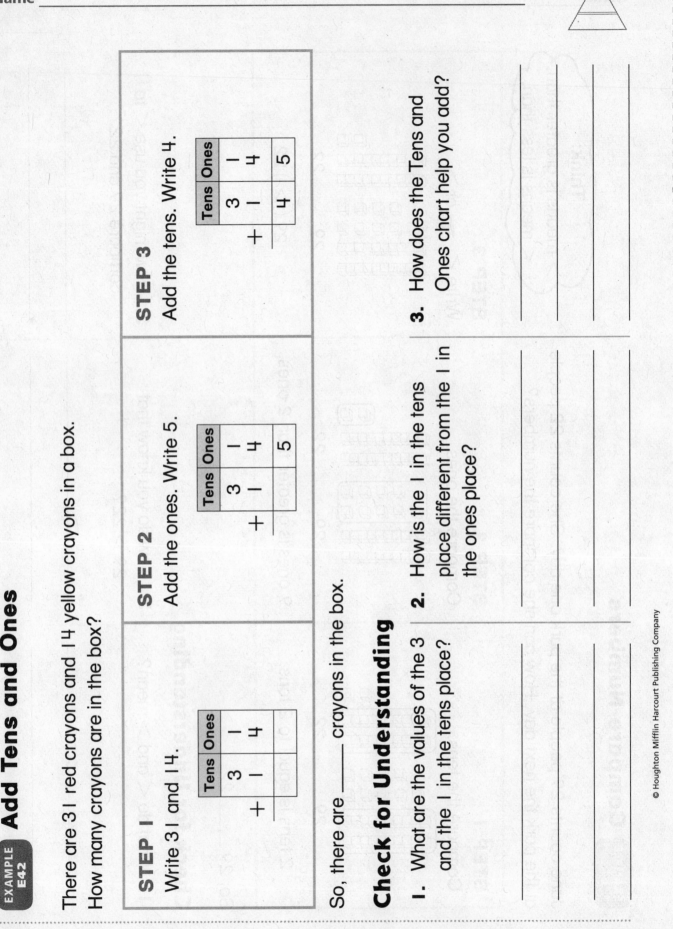

Add Tens and Ones

There are 31 red crayons and 14 yellow crayons in a box.
How many crayons are in the box?

STEP 1

Write 31 and 14.

Tens	Ones
3	1
1	4
+	

STEP 2

Add the ones. Write 5.

Tens	Ones
3	1
1	4
+	5

STEP 3

Add the tens. Write 4.

Tens	Ones
3	1
1	4
+	5
4	5

So, there are _____ crayons in the box.

Check for Understanding

1. What are the values of the 3 and the 1 in the tens place?

   _____

   _____

2. How is the 1 in the tens place different from the 1 in the ones place?

   _____

   _____

3. How does the Tens and Ones chart help you add?

   _____

   _____

   _____

EXAMPLE E43

Add On Tens

Jan 27 stickers.

She buys 20 more stickers.

How many stickers does Jan have now?

STEP 1

Show 27 + 20.

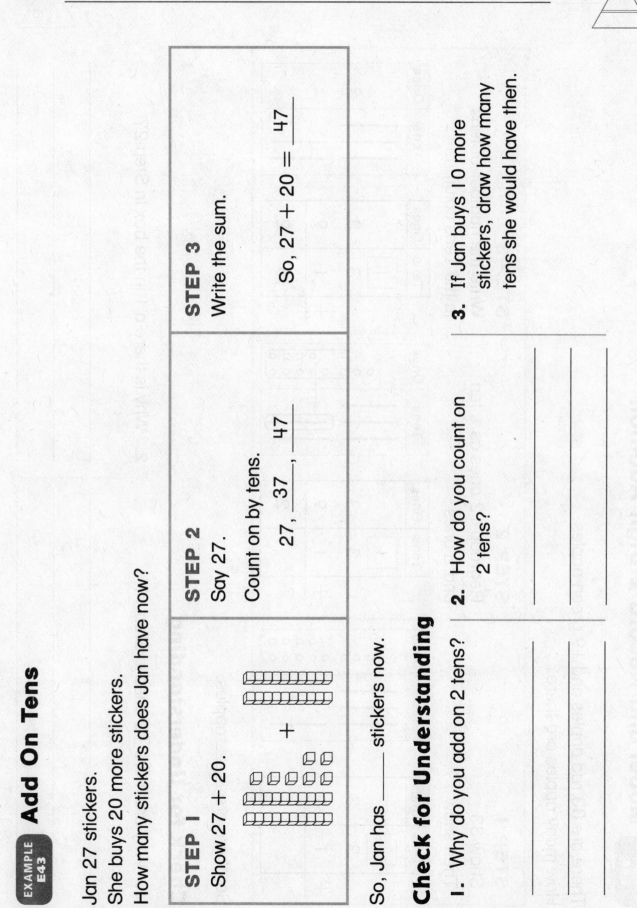

STEP 2

Say 27.

Count on by tens.

27, ___37___ , ___47___

STEP 3

Write the sum.

So, 27 + 20 = ___47___

So, Jan has ___ stickers now.

Check for Understanding

1. Why do you add on 2 tens?

_____

_____

2. How do you count on 2 tens?

_____

_____

3. If Jan buys 10 more stickers, draw how many tens she would have then.

Model and Record 2-Digit Addition

EXAMPLE
E44

There are 33 red apples and 19 green apples.
How many apples are there?

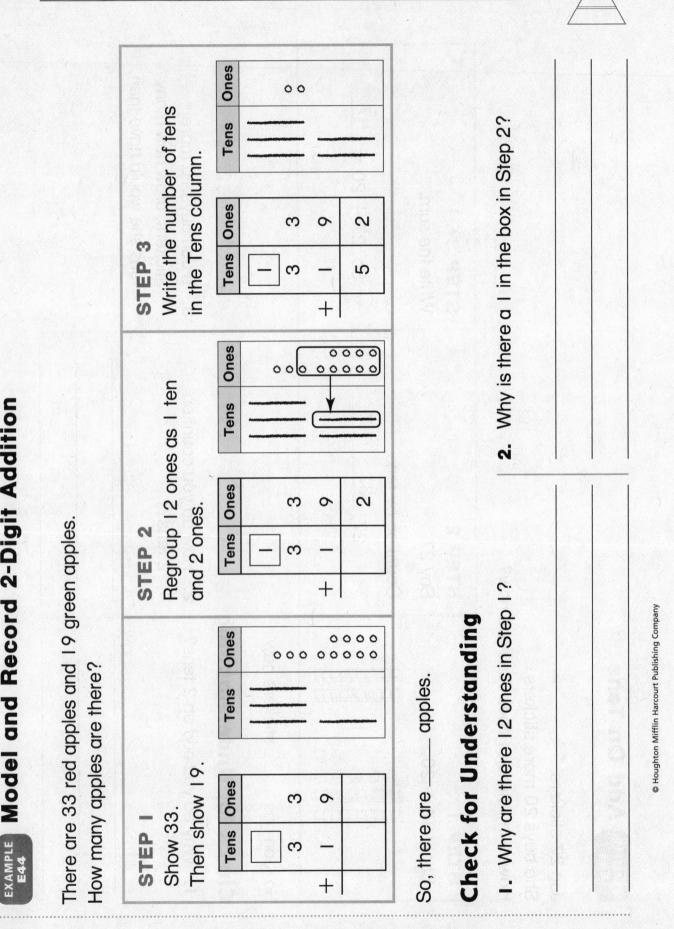

STEP 1

Show 33.
Then show 19.

Tens	Ones
☐ 3	3
1	9
+	

STEP 2

Regroup 12 ones as 1 ten
and 2 ones.

Tens	Ones
☐ 1 ☐ 3	3
1	9
+	2

STEP 3

Write the number of tens
in the Tens column.

Tens	Ones
☐ 1 ☐ 3	3
1	9
+ 5	2

So, there are _____ apples.

Check for Understanding

1. Why are there 12 ones in Step 1?

_____

_____

2. Why is there a 1 in the box in Step 2?

_____

_____

_____

EXAMPLE E45

Practice 2-Digit Addition

Ella sold 47 pencils in one week. She sold 25 pencils the next week.
How many pencils did Ella sell in both weeks?

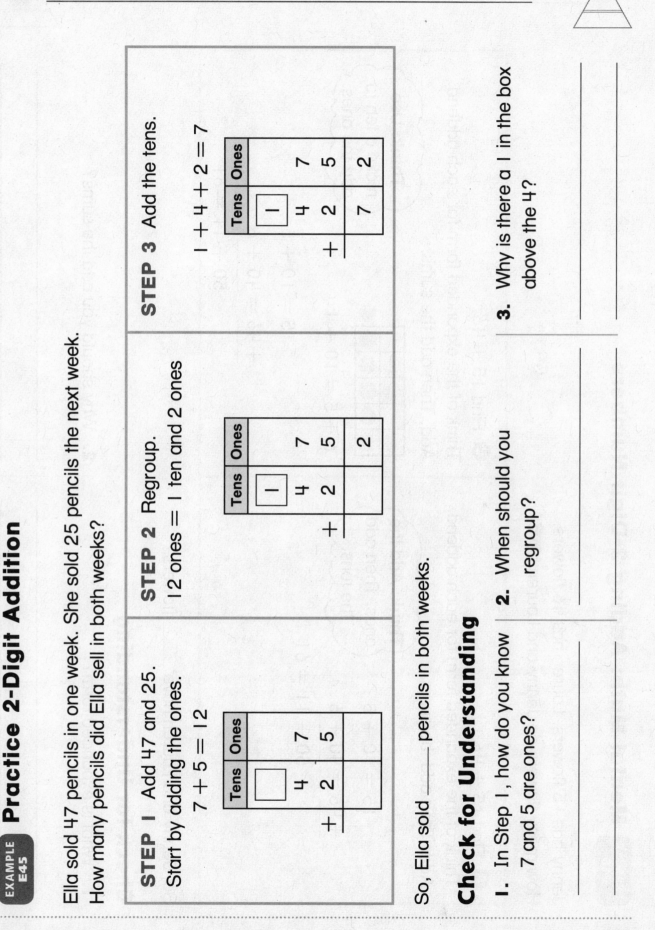

STEP 1 Add 47 and 25.
Start by adding the ones.

$7 + 5 = 12$

Tens	Ones
☐	
4	7
2	5
+	

STEP 2 Regroup.
12 ones = 1 ten and 2 ones

Tens	Ones
1	
4	7
2	5
+	2

STEP 3 Add the tens.

$1 + 4 + 2 = 7$

Tens	Ones
1	
4	7
2	5
+ 7	2

So, Ella sold _____ pencils in both weeks.

Check for Understanding

1. In Step 1, how do you know
   7 and 5 are ones?

   _____

2. When should you
   regroup?

   _____

3. Why is there a 1 in the box
   above the 4?

   _____

EXAMPLE E46 Mental Math: Adding 2-Digit Numbers

Jenny has 15 flowers. Lauren has 46 flowers.
How many flowers do Jenny and Lauren have?

A Find $15 + 46$.

Think of the expanded form for each addend.
Add. Then add the sums.

> **Think:** Add the ones. Then add the tens.

$$15 = 10 + 5$$
$$+46 = 40 + 6$$
$$\overline{50 + 11} = 61$$

B Find $15 + 46$.

Think of the expanded form for each addend.
Add. Then add the sums.

> **Think:** Use make a ten to add the ones.

$6 + 5 = 10 + 1$

$$15 = 10 + 5$$
$$+46 = 40 + 6$$
$$\overline{50 + 11} = 61$$

So, Jenny and Lauren have _____ flowers.

Check for Understanding

1. What is expanded form?

_____

2. Why should you add the sums?

_____

EXAMPLE E47

Ten Less

Gina has 24 raisins. She eats 10 of them.
How many raisins does Gina have left?

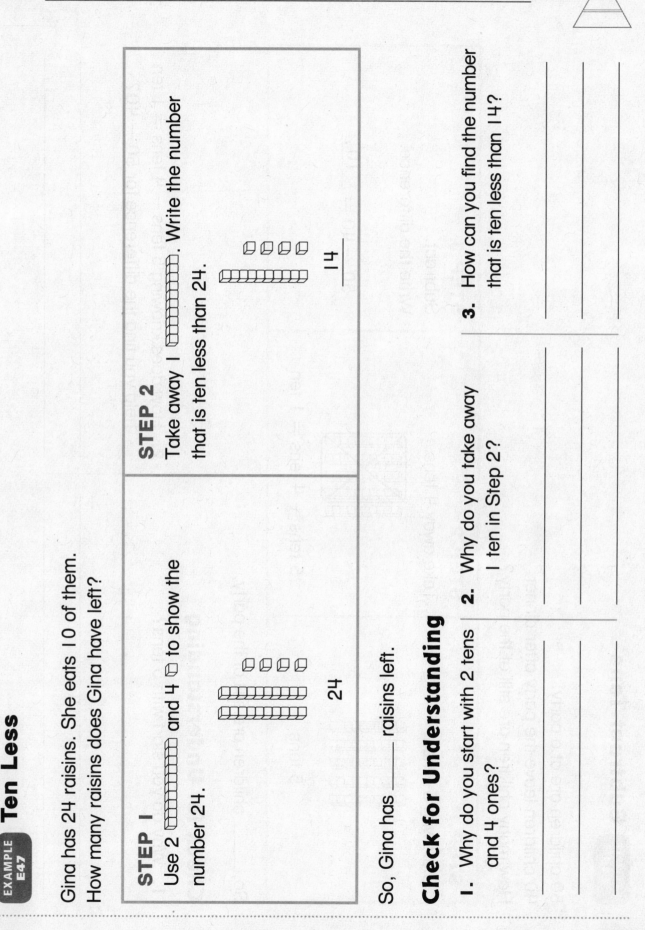

STEP 1

Use 2 ▭ and 4 ▯ to show the
number 24.

24

STEP 2

Take away 1 ▭. Write the number
that is ten less than 24.

14

So, Gina has _____ raisins left.

Check for Understanding

1. Why do you start with 2 tens
   and 4 ones?

2. Why do you take away
   1 ten in Step 2?

3. How can you find the number
   that is ten less than 14?

_____

_____

_____

Subtract Tens

50 children are at a party.
40 children leave the party after dinner.
How many children are still at the party?

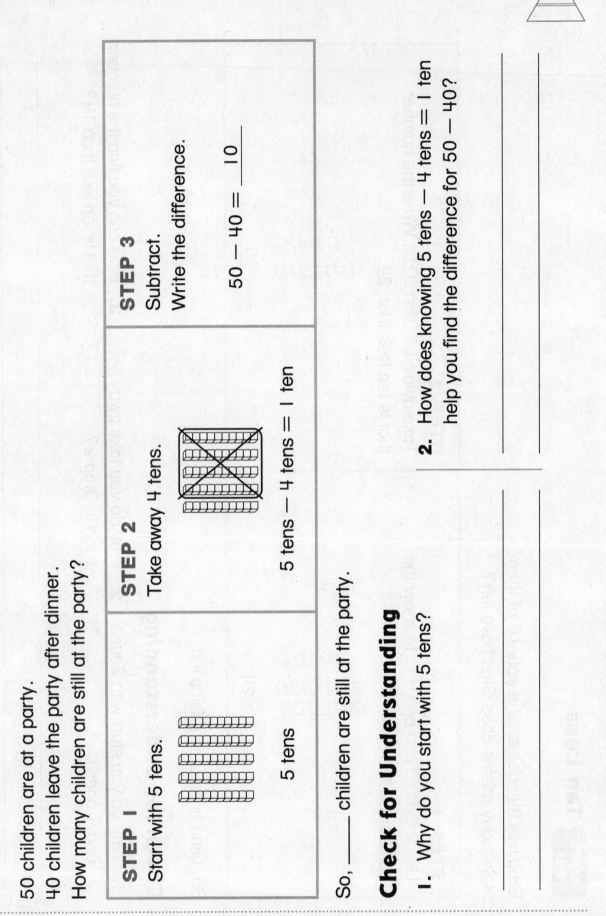

STEP I

Start with 5 tens.

5 tens

STEP 2

Take away 4 tens.

5 tens — 4 tens = I ten

STEP 3

Subtract.
Write the difference.

50 — 40 = _10_

So, _____ children are still at the party.

Check for Understanding

1. Why do you start with 5 tens?

_____

_____

2. How does knowing 5 tens — 4 tens = I ten
help you find the difference for 50 — 40?

_____

_____

EXAMPLE E49 Subtract Tens and Ones

There are 17 bananas. Ray eats 2 of the bananas.
How many bananas are there now?

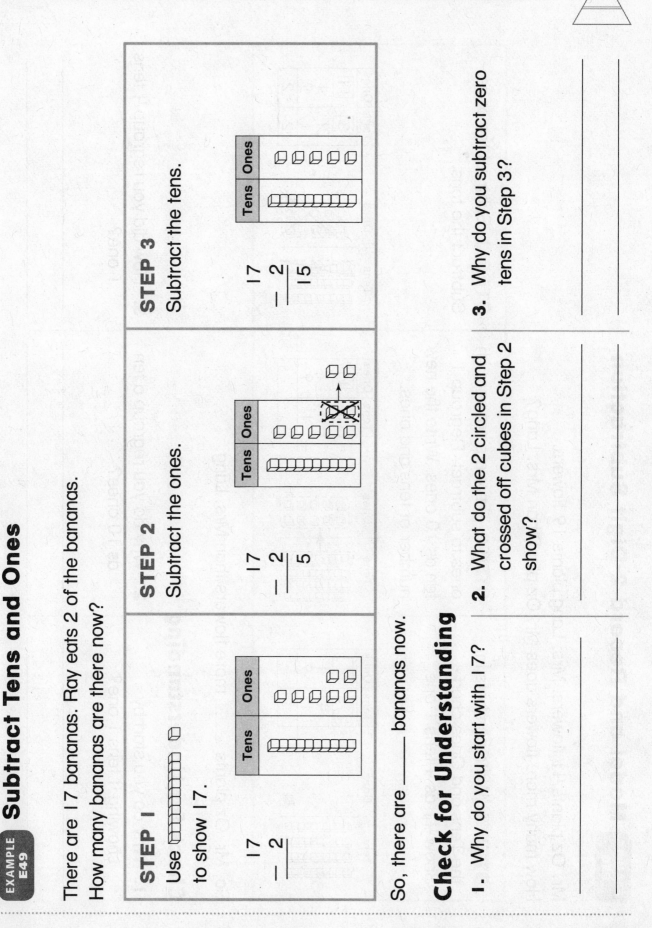

STEP 1

Use ▭▭▭▭▭▭▭▭▭ ▭ to show 17.

Tens	Ones

$$\begin{array}{r} 17 \\ -\ 2 \\ \hline \end{array}$$

STEP 2

Subtract the ones.

Tens	Ones

$$\begin{array}{r} 17 \\ -\ 2 \\ \hline 5 \end{array}$$

STEP 3

Subtract the tens.

Tens	Ones

$$\begin{array}{r} 17 \\ -\ 2 \\ \hline 15 \end{array}$$

So, there are _____ bananas now.

Check for Understanding

1. Why do you start with 17?

2. What do the 2 circled and crossed off cubes in Step 2 show?

3. Why do you subtract zero tens in Step 3?

EXAMPLE E50

Model and Record 2-Digit Subtraction

Mr. Oz plants 41 flowers. Mrs. Lang plants 19 flowers.
How many more flowers does Mr. Oz plant than Mrs. Lang?

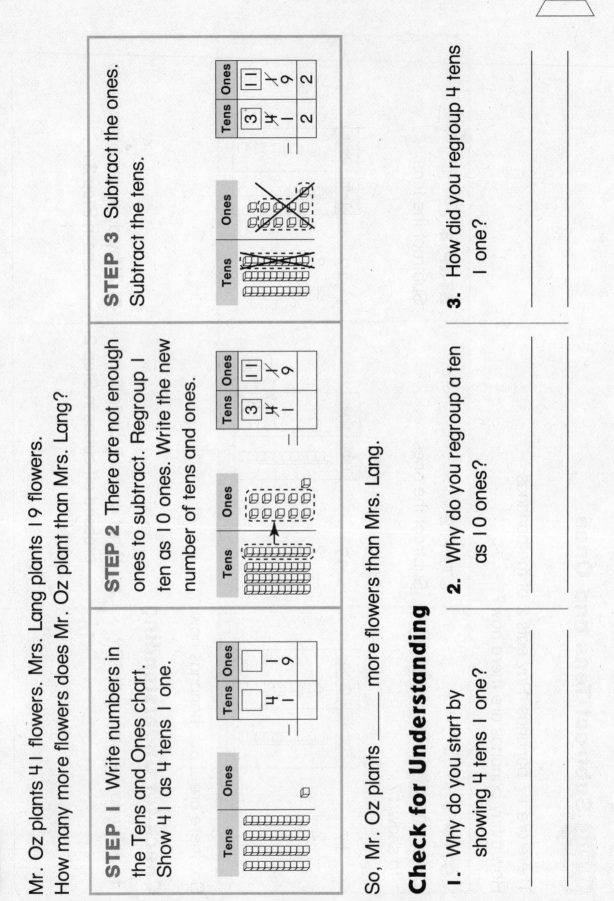

STEP 1 Write numbers in the Tens and Ones chart. Show 41 as 4 tens 1 one.

STEP 2 There are not enough ones to subtract. Regroup 1 ten as 10 ones. Write the new number of tens and ones.

STEP 3 Subtract the ones. Subtract the tens.

So, Mr. Oz plants _____ more flowers than Mrs. Lang.

Check for Understanding

1. Why do you start by showing 4 tens 1 one?

_____

2. Why do you regroup a ten as 10 ones?

_____

3. How did you regroup 4 tens 1 one?

_____

© Houghton Mifflin Harcourt Publishing Company

Name _____

Model Regrouping for Addition

There are 27 berries in one bowl. There are 15 berries in a different bowl. How many berries are in the bowls?

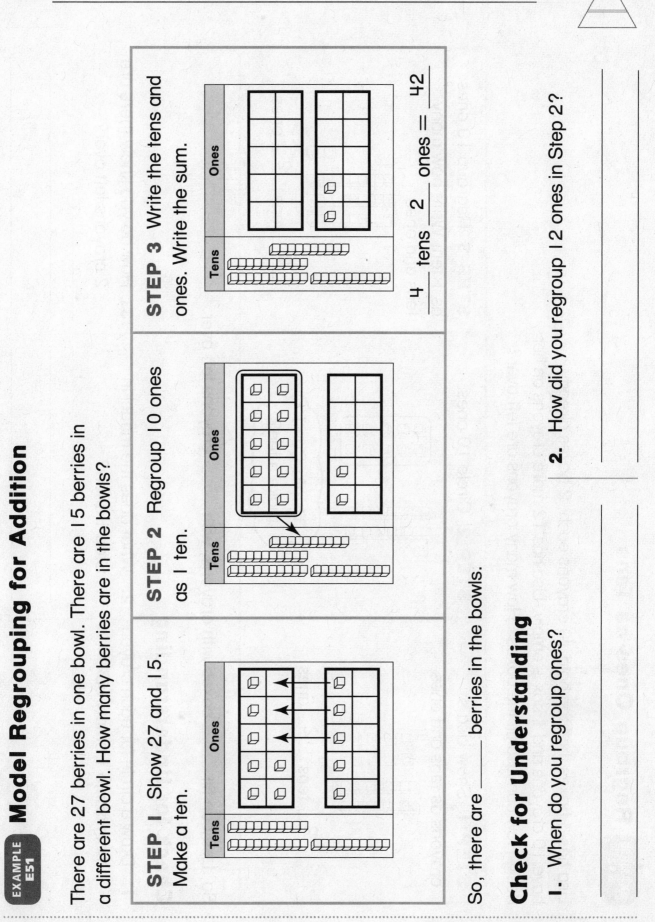

STEP 1 Show 27 and 15. Make a ten.

Tens	Ones

STEP 2 Regroup 10 ones as 1 ten.

Tens	Ones

STEP 3 Write the tens and ones. Write the sum.

Tens	Ones

4 tens 2 ones = 42

So, there are _____ berries in the bowls.

Check for Understanding

1. When do you regroup ones?

_____

2. How did you regroup 12 ones in Step 2?

_____

E52

Regroup Ones as Tens

Lisa has 3 boxes that can hold 10 crayons each. 2 boxes already have 10 crayons and 1 box is empty. Lisa has 12 more crayons on her desk. How can Lisa fill the boxes? How many crayons are left over?

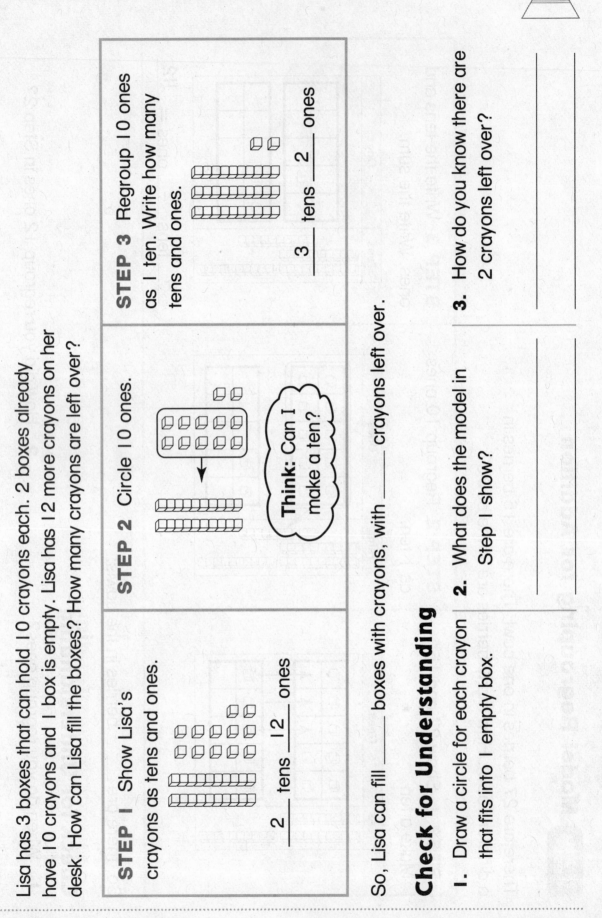

STEP 1 Show Lisa's crayons as tens and ones.

_2_ tens _12_ ones

STEP 2 Circle 10 ones.

Think: Can I make a ten?

STEP 3 Regroup 10 ones as 1 ten. Write how many tens and ones.

_3_ tens _2_ ones

So, Lisa can fill _____ boxes with crayons, with _____ crayons left over.

Check for Understanding

1. Draw a circle for each crayon that fits into 1 empty box.

2. What does the model in Step 1 show?

_____

_____

3. How do you know there are 2 crayons left over?

_____

_____

Name _____

EXAMPLE
E53

Model Adding Two 2-Digit Numbers with Regrouping

Juan has 15 buttons in one jar. He has 16 buttons in another jar. How many buttons does Juan have?

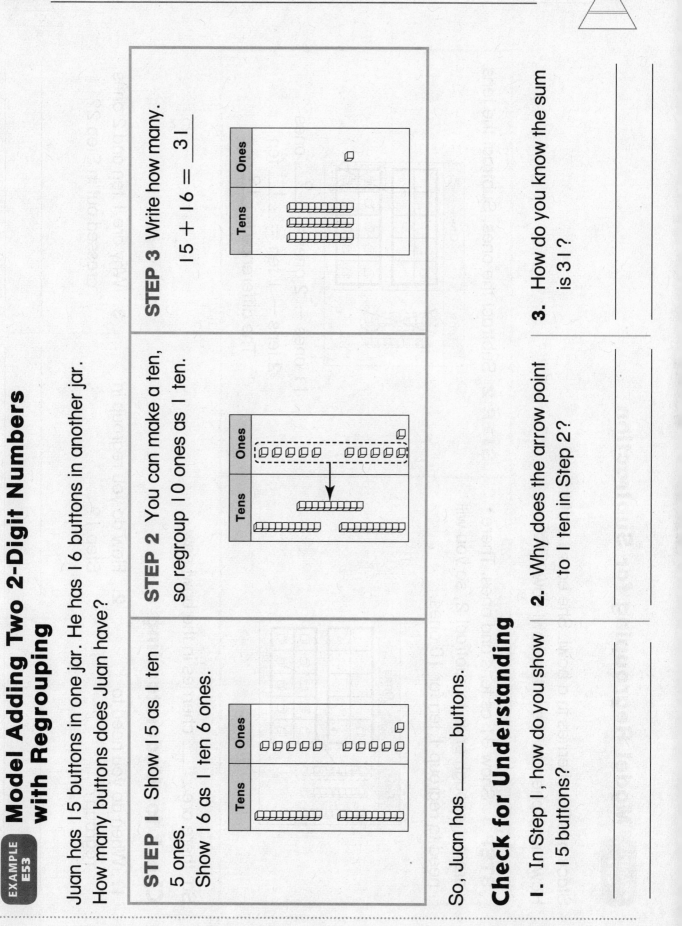

STEP 1 Show 15 as 1 ten 5 ones.
Show 16 as 1 ten 6 ones.

Tens	Ones

STEP 2 You can make a ten, so regroup 10 ones as 1 ten.

Tens	Ones

STEP 3 Write how many.

15 + 16 = ___31___

Tens	Ones

So, Juan has _____ buttons.

Check for Understanding

1. In Step 1, how do you show 15 buttons?

2. Why does the arrow point to 1 ten in Step 2?

3. How do you know the sum is 31?

EXAMPLE E54 Model Regrouping for Subtraction

Stacy has 31 cherries in a bowl. She eats 12 of them.
How many cherries are in the bowl now?

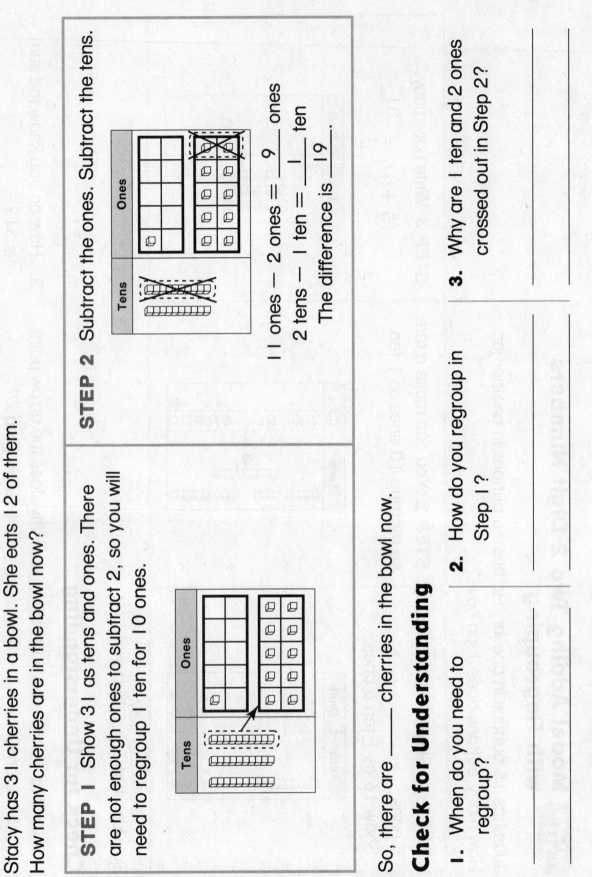

STEP 1 Show 31 as tens and ones. There are not enough ones to subtract 2, so you will need to regroup 1 ten for 10 ones.

STEP 2 Subtract the ones. Subtract the tens.

11 ones − 2 ones = ____9___ ones

2 tens − 1 ten = ____1___ ten

The difference is ___19___.

So, there are _____ cherries in the bowl now.

Check for Understanding

1. When do you need to regroup?

_____

2. How do you regroup in Step 1?

_____

3. Why are 1 ten and 2 ones crossed out in Step 2?

_____

EXAMPLE
E55

Regroup Tens as Ones

Ed has 2 boxes of pens. Each box has 10 pens in it.
He also has 1 pen in his desk. Ed moves all the pens from
one box to his desk. How can Ed describe his pens now?

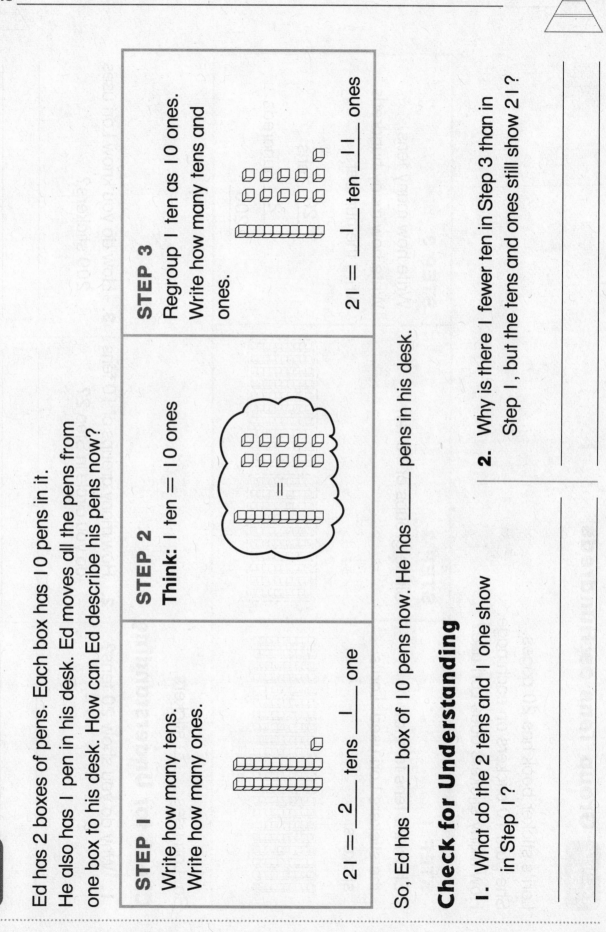

STEP 1

Write how many tens.
Write how many ones.

21 = __2__ tens __1__ one

STEP 2

Think: 1 ten = 10 ones

=

So, Ed has _____ box of 10 pens now. He has _____ pens in his desk.

STEP 3

Regroup 1 ten as 10 ones.
Write how many tens and ones.

21 = __1__ ten __11__ ones

Check for Understanding

1. What do the 2 tens and 1 one show
   in Step 1?

_____

_____

2. Why is there 1 fewer ten in Step 3 than in
   Step 1, but the tens and ones still show 21?

_____

_____

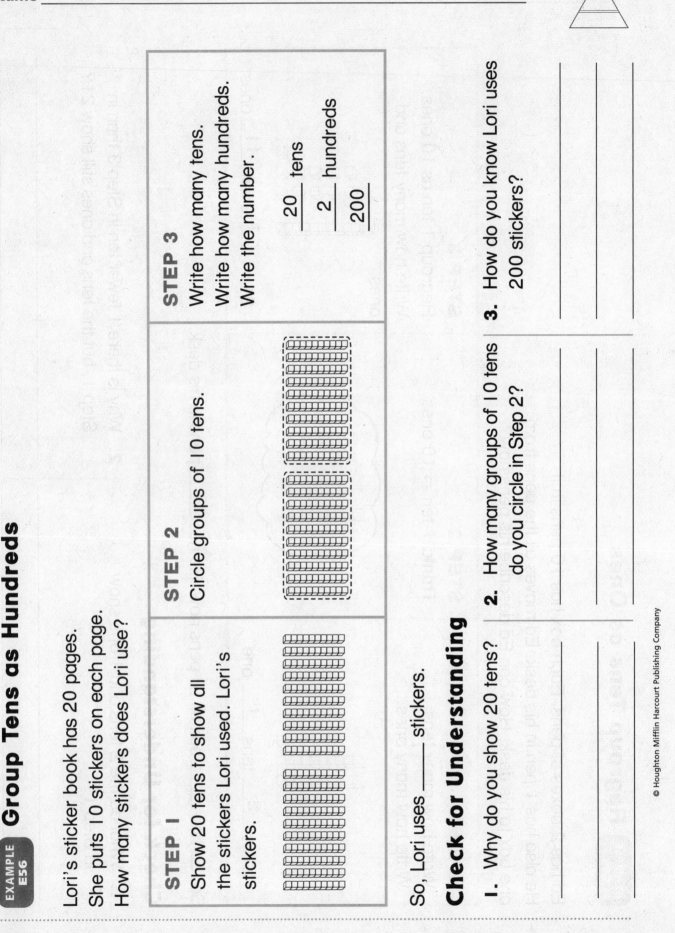

EXAMPLE E56 **Group Tens as Hundreds**

Lori's sticker book has 20 pages.
She puts 10 stickers on each page.
How many stickers does Lori use?

STEP 1

Show 20 tens to show all
the stickers Lori used. Lori's
stickers.

STEP 2

Circle groups of 10 tens.

STEP 3

Write how many tens.
Write how many hundreds.
Write the number.

20 tens
2 hundreds
200

So, Lori uses _____ stickers.

Check for Understanding

1. Why do you show 20 tens?

_____

_____

2. How many groups of 10 tens
do you circle in Step 2?

_____

_____

3. How do you know Lori uses
200 stickers?

_____

_____

_____

Name _____

EXAMPLE E57

Count On and Count Back by 10 and 100

Amy recycled 225 bottles this year. Last year she recycled 100 fewer bottles. How many bottles did Amy recycle last year?

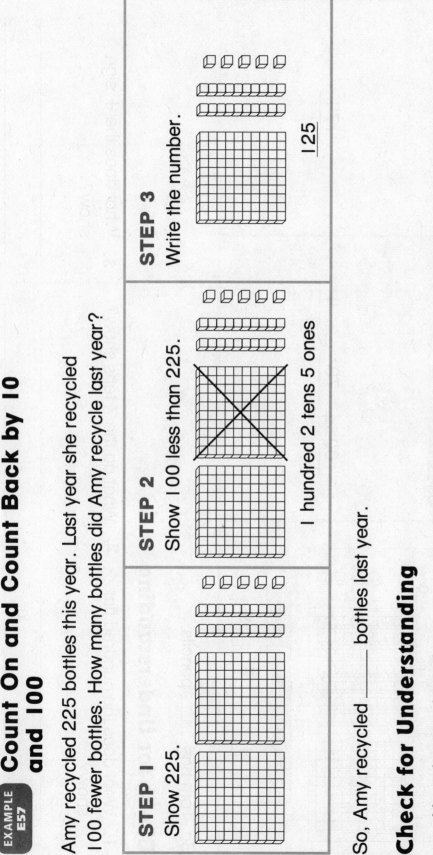

STEP 1

Show 225.

STEP 2

Show 100 less than 225.

1 hundred 2 tens 5 ones

STEP 3

Write the number.

125

So, Amy recycled _____ bottles last year.

Check for Understanding

1. How do you show the number 225?

    _____
    _____
    _____

2. Why is there an X on one of the hundreds in Step 2?

3. Amy's friend recycled 10 fewer bottles than Amy this year. Draw to show 10 less than 225.

EXAMPLE E58 — Hundreds, Tens, and Ones

Each box has 100 pencils. Each pack has 10 pencils. Tom has 1 box, 7 packs, and 4 extra pencils. How many pencils does Tom have?

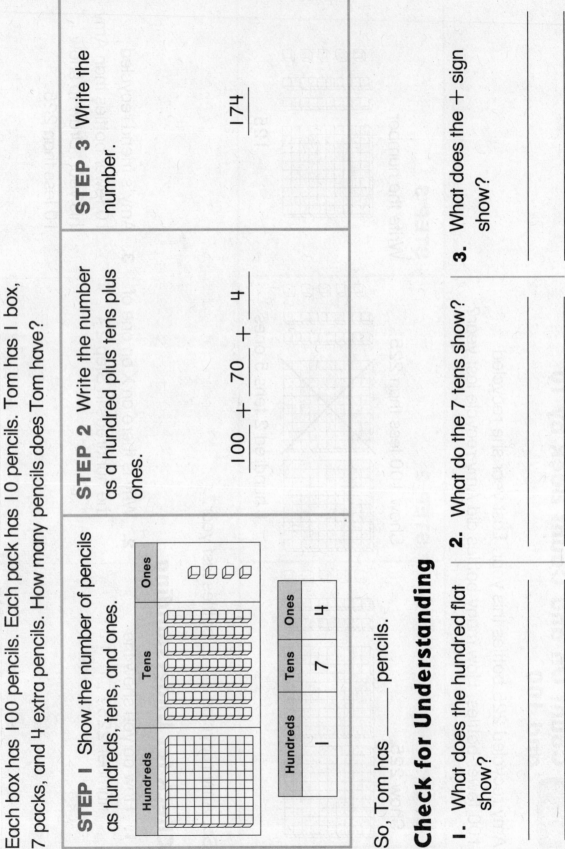

STEP 1 Show the number of pencils as hundreds, tens, and ones.

Hundreds	Tens	Ones
1	7	4

STEP 2 Write the number as a hundred plus tens plus ones.

$$\underline{100} + \underline{70} + \underline{4}$$

STEP 3 Write the number.

$$\underline{174}$$

So, Tom has _____ pencils.

Check for Understanding

1. What does the hundred flat show?

   _____

2. What do the 7 tens show?

   _____

3. What does the + sign show?

   _____

EXAMPLE E59 Explore 3-Digit Numbers

Jacob has 12 bags of marbles. There are 10 marbles in each bag. How many marbles does Jacob have?

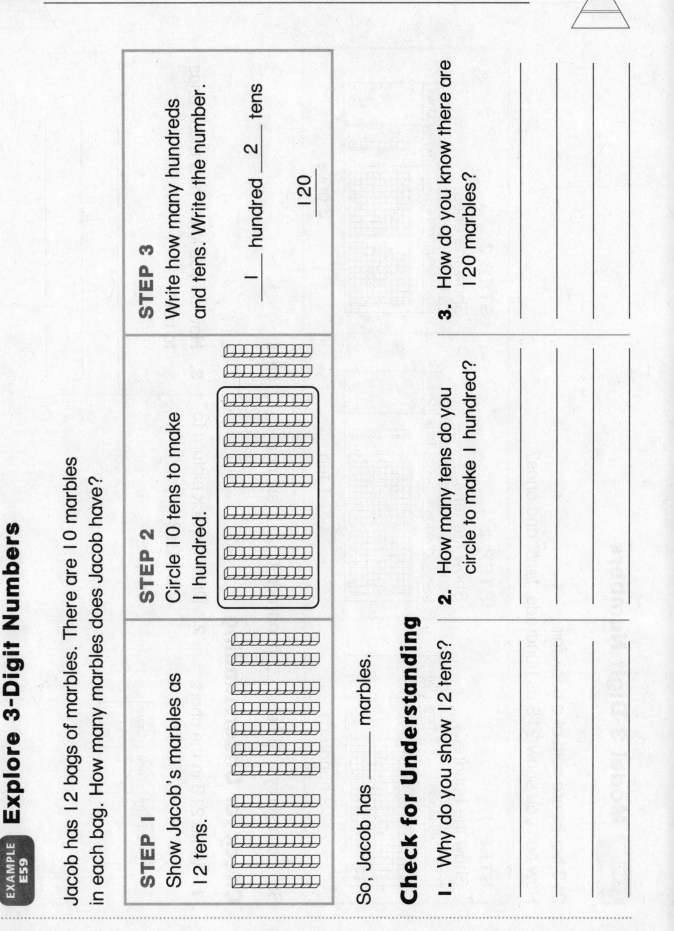

STEP 1

Show Jacob's marbles as 12 tens.

STEP 2

Circle 10 tens to make 1 hundred.

STEP 3

Write how many hundreds and tens. Write the number.

__1__ hundred __2__ tens

__120__

So, Jacob has _____ marbles.

Check for Understanding

1. Why do you show 12 tens?

_____

_____

_____

2. How many tens do you circle to make 1 hundred?

_____

_____

_____

3. How do you know there are 120 marbles?

_____

_____

_____

EXAMPLE
E60

Model 3-Digit Numbers

213 books are sold at a book fair.

How can you show 213 as hundreds, tens, and ones?

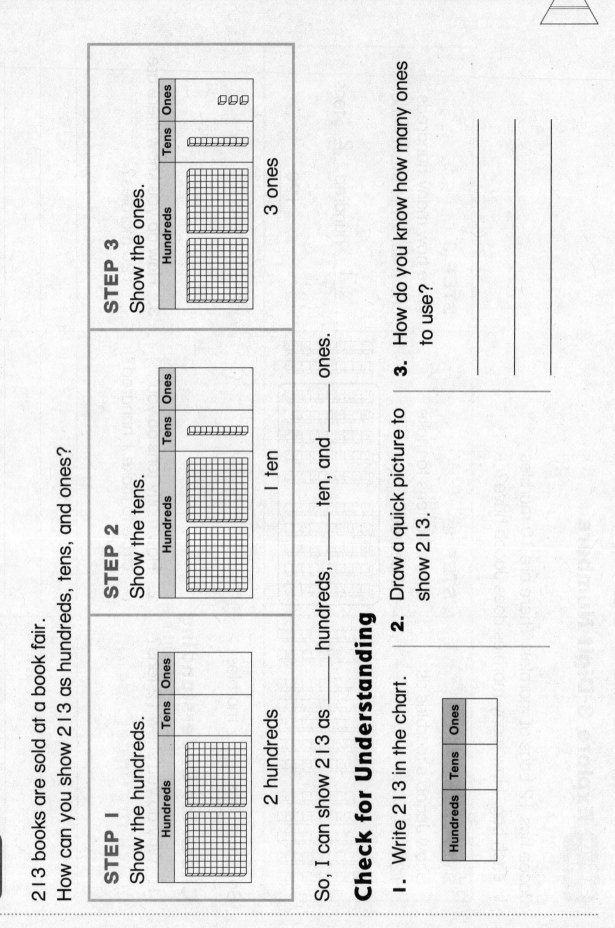

STEP 1
Show the hundreds.

Hundreds	Tens	Ones

2 hundreds

STEP 2
Show the tens.

Hundreds	Tens	Ones

1 ten

STEP 3
Show the ones.

Hundreds	Tens	Ones

3 ones

So, I can show 213 as ____ hundreds, ____ ten, and ____ ones.

Check for Understanding

1. Write 213 in the chart.

Hundreds	Tens	Ones

2. Draw a quick picture to show 213.

3. How do you know how many ones to use?

_____

_____

_____

© Houghton Mifflin Harcourt Publishing Company

Name _____

EXAMPLE E61

Draw to Represent 3-Digit Addition

On Friday, 124 people go to see a play. On Saturday, 143 people go to see the play. How many people see the play in the two days?

STEP 1

Draw quick pictures of 124 and 143.

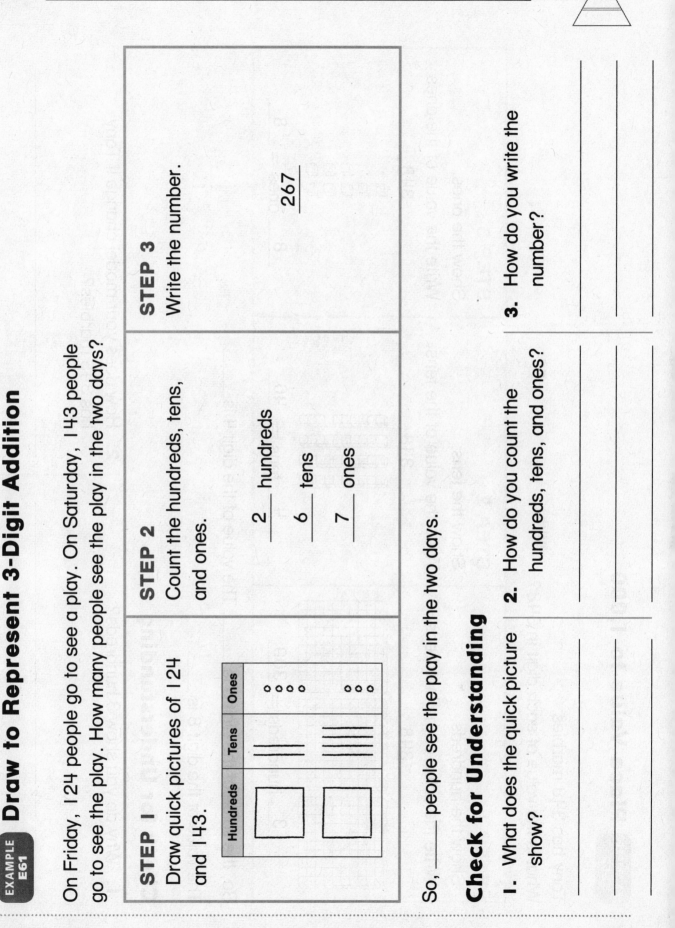

Hundreds	Tens	Ones
□ □	‒ ‒	○ ○ ○ ○
	‒ ‒ ‒ ‒	○ ○ ○

STEP 2

Count the hundreds, tens, and ones.

_2_ hundreds

_6_ tens

_7_ ones

STEP 3

Write the number.

_267_

So, ____ people see the play in the two days.

Check for Understanding

1. What does the quick picture show?

2. How do you count the hundreds, tens, and ones?

3. How do you write the number?

EXAMPLE E62

Place Value to 1,000

Tony has 348 marbles.

What is the value of each digit in 348?

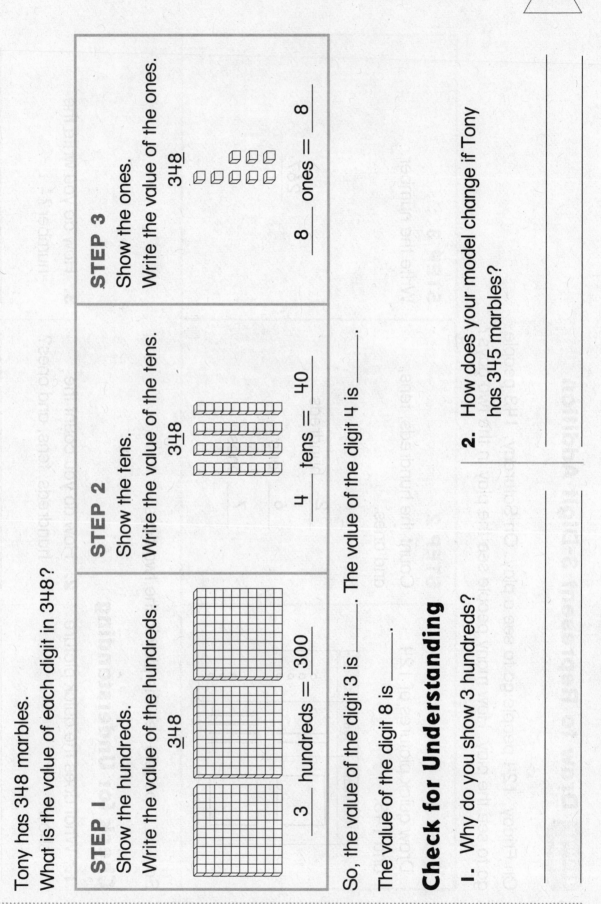

STEP 1

Show the hundreds.

Write the value of the hundreds.

34<u>8</u>

___3___ hundreds = ___300___

STEP 2

Show the tens.

Write the value of the tens.

3<u>4</u>8

___4___ tens = ___40___

STEP 3

Show the ones.

Write the value of the ones.

34<u>8</u>

___8___ ones = ___8___

So, the value of the digit 3 is _____. The value of the digit 4 is _____.

The value of the digit 8 is _____.

Check for Understanding

1. Why do you show 3 hundreds?

2. How does your model change if Tony has 345 marbles?

EXAMPLE E63

3-Digit Addition: Regroup Ones

Suzie plants 218 yellow daisies and 135 white daisies in her garden. How many daisies does Suzie plant?

STEP 1

Add the ones. $8 + 5 = \underline{13}$

Regroup 10 ones as 1 ten.

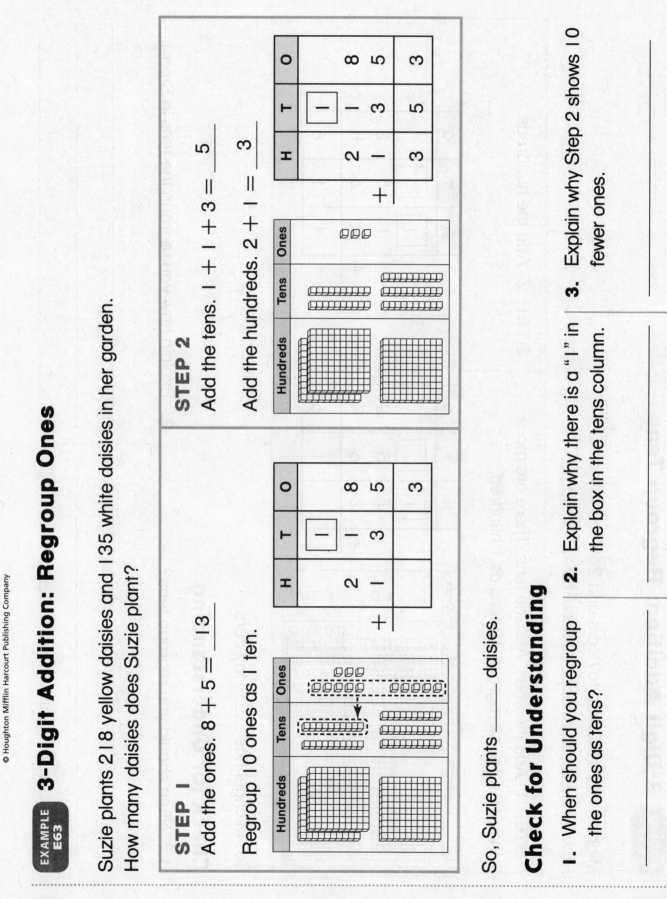

H	T	O
	☐1	
2	1	8
+1	3	5
		3

STEP 2

Add the tens. $1 + 1 + 3 = \underline{5}$

Add the hundreds. $2 + 1 = \underline{3}$

H	T	O
	☐1	
2	1	8
+1	3	5
3	5	3

So, Suzie plants _____ daisies.

Check for Understanding

1. When should you regroup the ones as tens?

2. Explain why there is a "1" in the box in the tens column.

3. Explain why Step 2 shows 10 fewer ones.

3-Digit Addition: Regroup Tens

EXAMPLE E64

Michael has 152 blue toy cars and 264 red toy cars.
How many toy cars does Michael have?

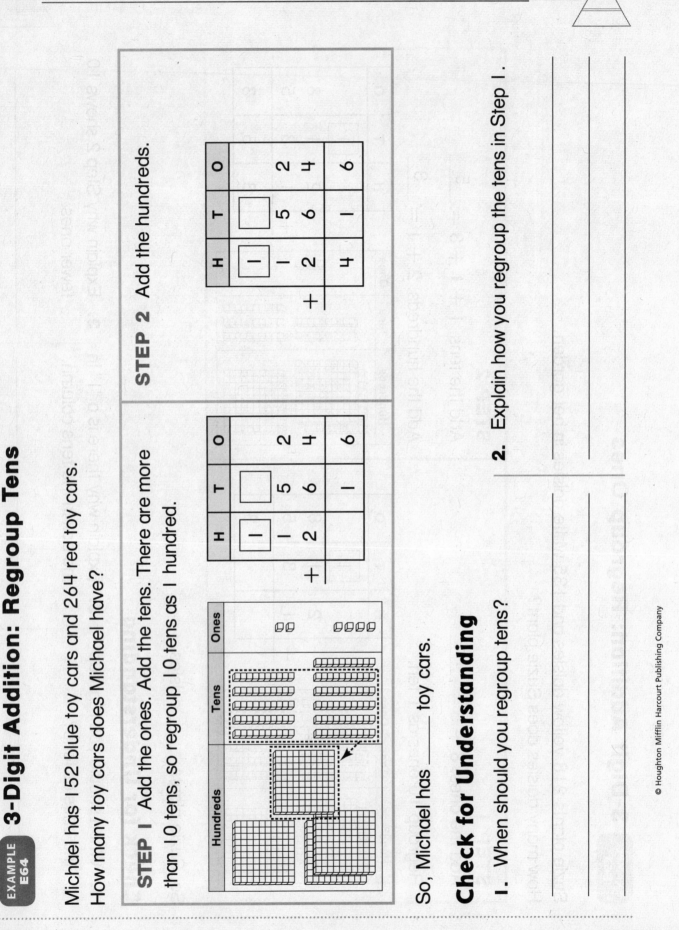

STEP 1 Add the ones. Add the tens. There are more than 10 tens, so regroup 10 tens as 1 hundred.

H	T	O
1	☐	
1	5	2
2	6	4
+		
	1	6

STEP 2 Add the hundreds.

H	T	O
1	☐	
1	5	2
2	6	4
+		
4	1	6

So, Michael has _____ toy cars.

Check for Understanding

1. When should you regroup tens?

_____

_____

2. Explain how you regroup the tens in Step 1.

_____

_____

EXAMPLE E65

3-Digit Subtraction: Regroup Tens

There are 255 pencils at a store. Then 129 of the pencils are sold. How many pencils are left?

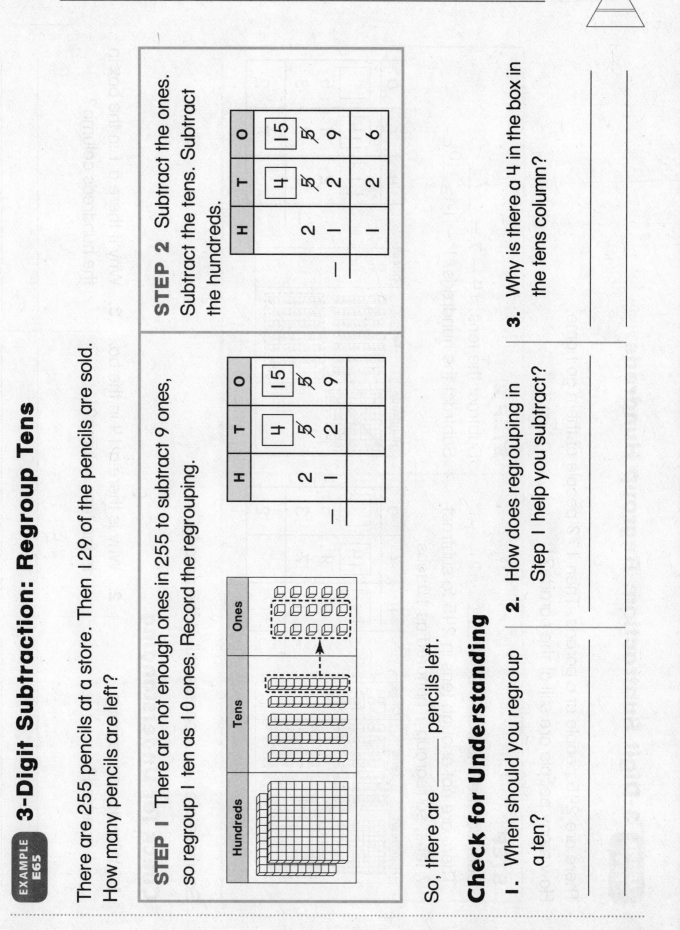

STEP 1 There are not enough ones in 255 to subtract 9 ones, so regroup 1 ten as 10 ones. Record the regrouping.

H	T	O
2	4 5̸	15 5̸
– 1	2	9

STEP 2 Subtract the ones. Subtract the tens. Subtract the hundreds.

H	T	O
2	4 5̸	15 5̸
– 1	2	9
1	2	6

So, there are _____ pencils left.

Check for Understanding

1. When should you regroup a ten?

2. How does regrouping in Step 1 help you subtract?

3. Why is there a 4 in the box in the tens column?

_____

_____

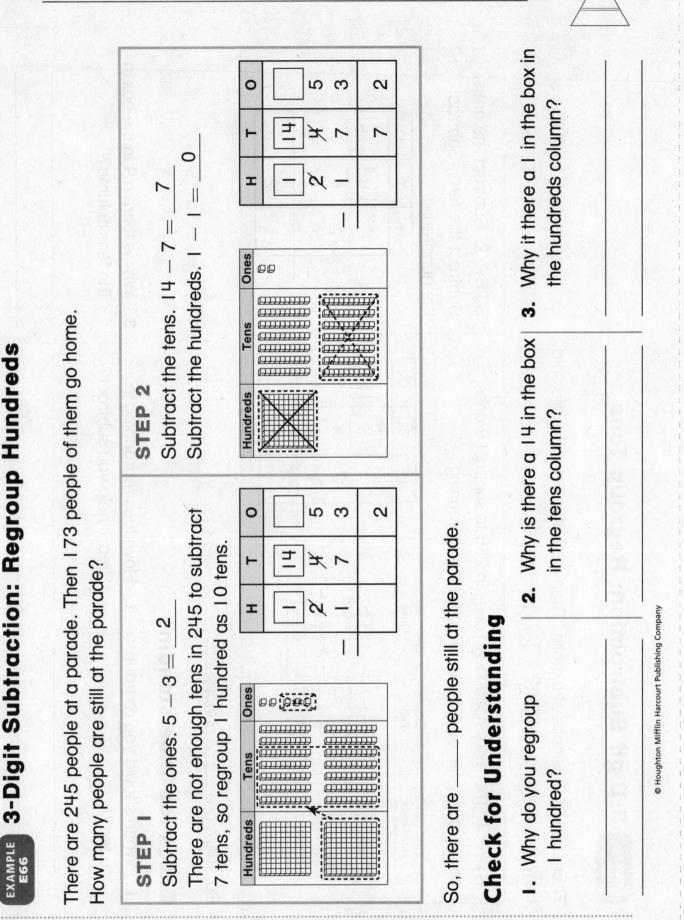

EXAMPLE
E66

3-Digit Subtraction: Regroup Hundreds

There are 245 people at a parade. Then 173 people of them go home. How many people are still at the parade?

STEP I

Subtract the ones. 5 − 3 = 2

There are not enough tens in 245 to subtract 7 tens, so regroup I hundred as 10 tens.

H	T	O
1̶2̶ 1	1̶4̶ 4	☐ 5
− 1	7	3
		2

STEP 2

Subtract the tens. 14 − 7 = 7
Subtract the hundreds. 1 − 1 = 0

H	T	O
1̶2̶ 1	1̶4̶ 4	☐ 5
− 1	7	3
0	7	2

So, there are _____ people still at the parade.

Check for Understanding

1. Why do you regroup I hundred?

_____

_____

2. Why is there a 14 in the box in the tens column?

_____

_____

3. Why it there a 1 in the box in the hundreds column?

_____

_____

EXAMPLE E67

Identify Two-Dimensional Shapes

Holly has this group of shapes.

How many squares does Holly have?

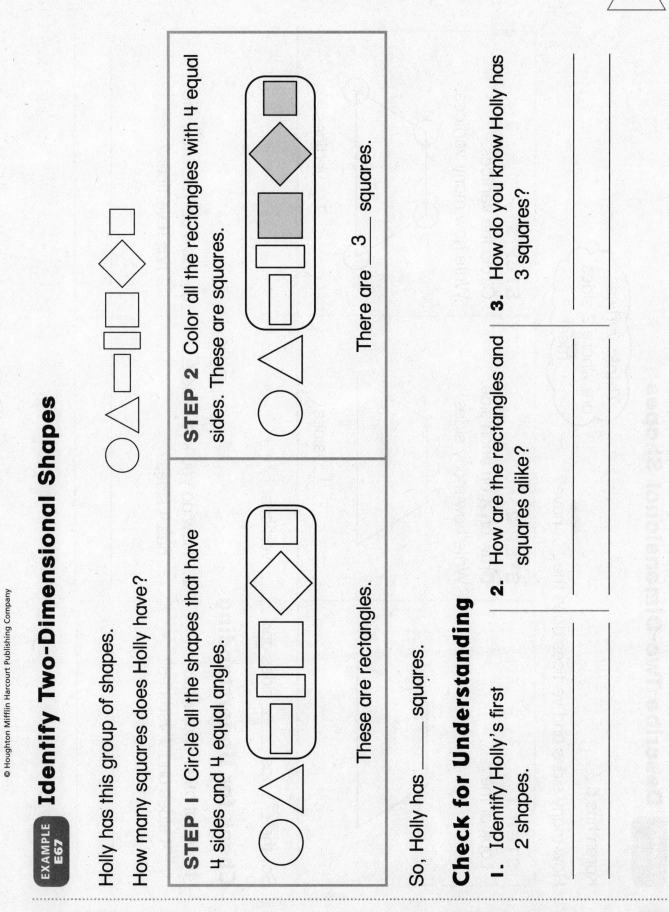

STEP 1 Circle all the shapes that have 4 sides and 4 equal angles.

These are rectangles.

STEP 2 Color all the rectangles with 4 equal sides. These are squares.

There are __3__ squares.

So, Holly has ____ squares.

Check for Understanding

1. Identify Holly's first 2 shapes.

_____

_____

2. How are the rectangles and squares alike?

_____

_____

3. How do you know Holly has 3 squares?

_____

_____

EXAMPLE E68

Describe Two-Dimensional Shapes

Think: vertices are where 2 sides meet

Karen has a △.

How many sides and vertices does the △ have?

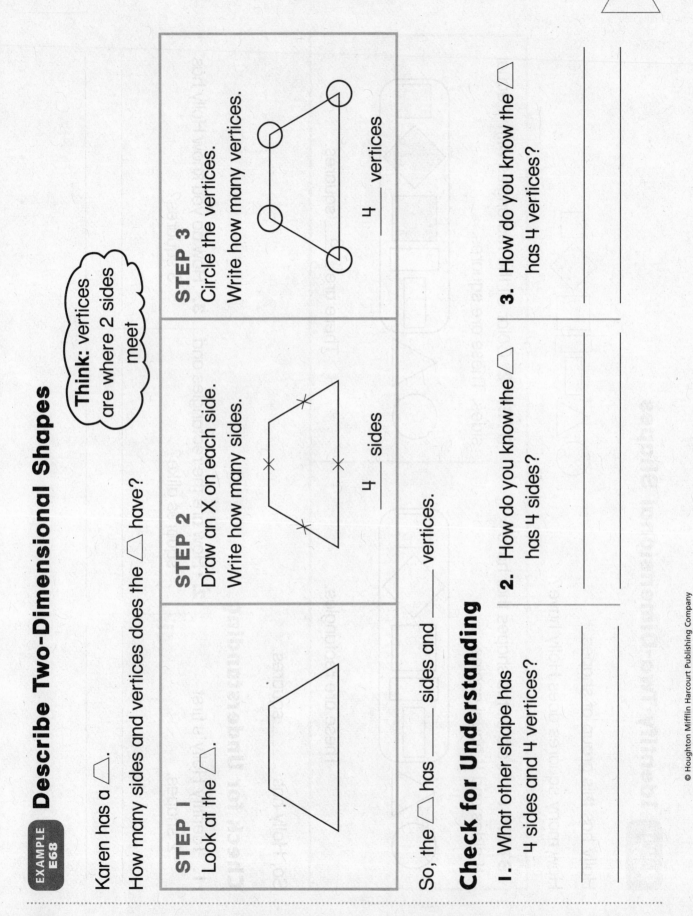

STEP 1

Look at the △.

STEP 2

Draw an X on each side.
Write how many sides.

4 ___ sides

STEP 3

Circle the vertices.
Write how many vertices.

4 ___ vertices

So, the △ has ____ sides and ____ vertices.

Check for Understanding

1. What other shape has 4 sides and 4 vertices?

_____

2. How do you know the △ has 4 sides?

_____

3. How do you know the △ has 4 vertices?

_____

EXAMPLE E69

Sort and Classify Two-Dimensional Shapes

Darrell has a set of shapes.
How can he sort his shapes by color and size?

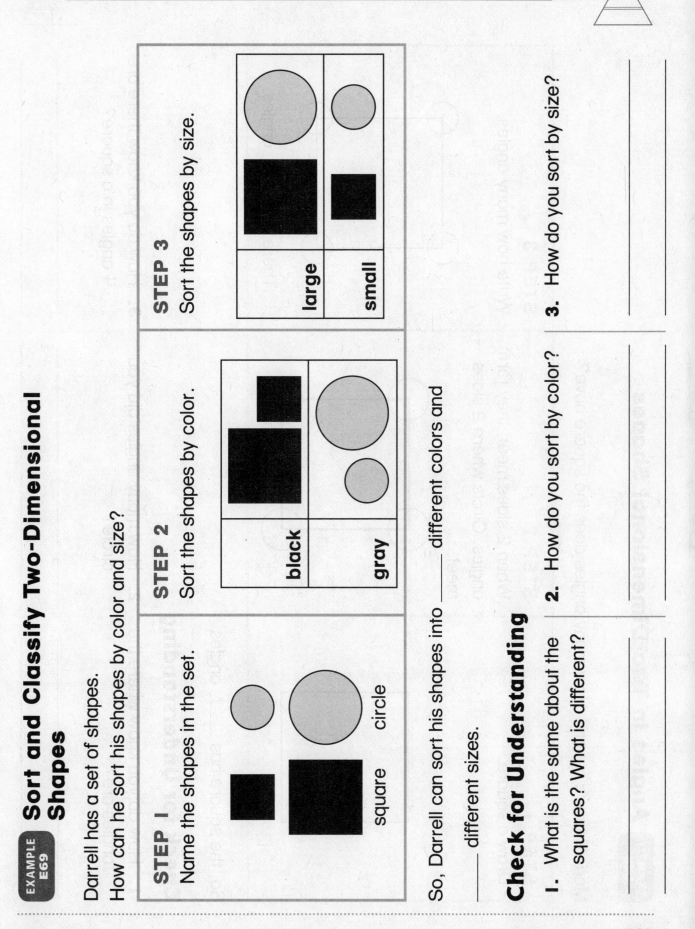

STEP 1
Name the shapes in the set.

square   circle

STEP 2
Sort the shapes by color.

black

gray

STEP 3
Sort the shapes by size.

large

small

So, Darrell can sort his shapes into ____ different colors and
____ different sizes.

Check for Understanding

1. What is the same about the squares? What is different?

2. How do you sort by color?

3. How do you sort by size?

EXAMPLE E70   Angles in Two-Dimensional Shapes

Mario draws a square. How many angles does the square have?

STEP 1
Draw a square.

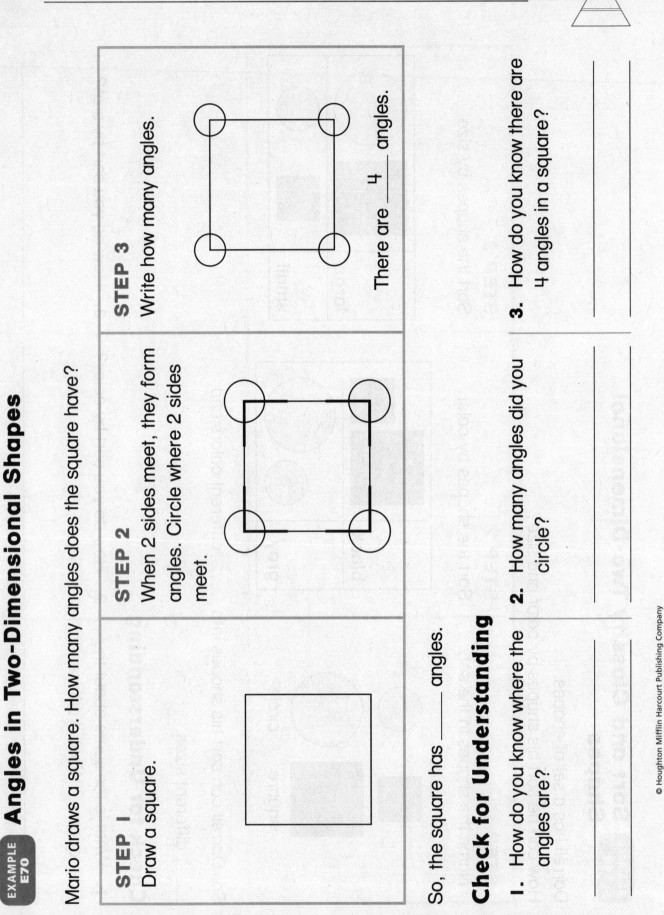

STEP 2
When 2 sides meet, they form angles. Circle where 2 sides meet.

STEP 3
Write how many angles.

There are __4__ angles.

So, the square has _____ angles.

Check for Understanding

1. How do you know where the angles are?

_____

_____

2. How many angles did you circle?

_____

_____

3. How do you know there are 4 angles in a square?

_____

_____

© Houghton Mifflin Harcourt Publishing Company

Identify Cones, Cylinders, and Spheres

Tia has 3 different solid shapes.

How can she tell which is the cone, the cylinder, or the sphere?

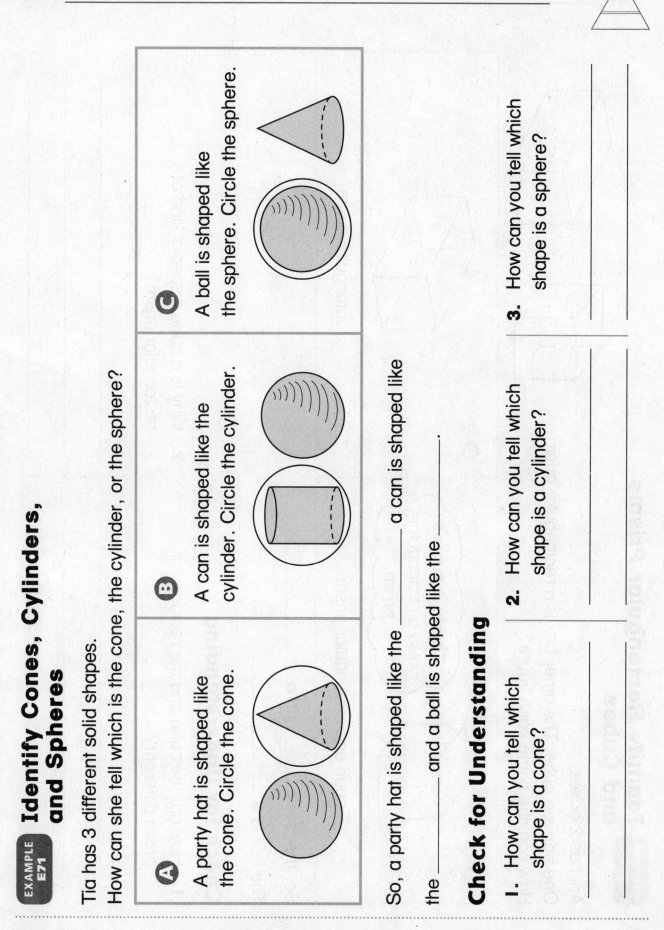

A A party hat is shaped like the cone. Circle the cone.

B A can is shaped like the cylinder. Circle the cylinder.

C A ball is shaped like the sphere. Circle the sphere.

So, a party hat is shaped like the _____ a can is shaped like the _____ and a ball is shaped like the _____.

Check for Understanding

1. How can you tell which shape is a cone?

_____

2. How can you tell which shape is a cylinder?

_____

3. How can you tell which shape is a sphere?

_____

© Houghton Mifflin Harcourt Publishing Company

EXAMPLE E72 Identify Rectangular Prisms and Cubes

Ani has 2 boxes.

One box is a cube. The other box is a rectangular prism.

How can she name each figure?

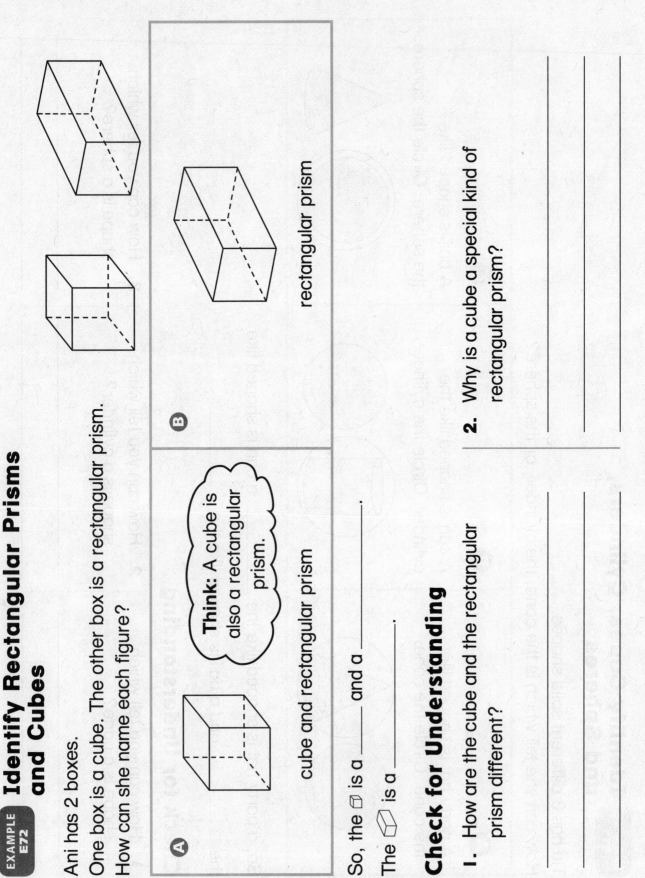

A

Think: A cube is also a rectangular prism.

cube and rectangular prism

B

rectangular prism

So, the ⬡ is a _____ and a _____ .

The ⬡ is a _____ .

Check for Understanding

1. How are the cube and the rectangular prism different?

_____

_____

2. Why is a cube a special kind of rectangular prism?

_____

_____

E72

EXAMPLE E73

Equal Parts

Sally has a circle that is cut into equal parts.
Which picture below shows her circle cut into equal parts?

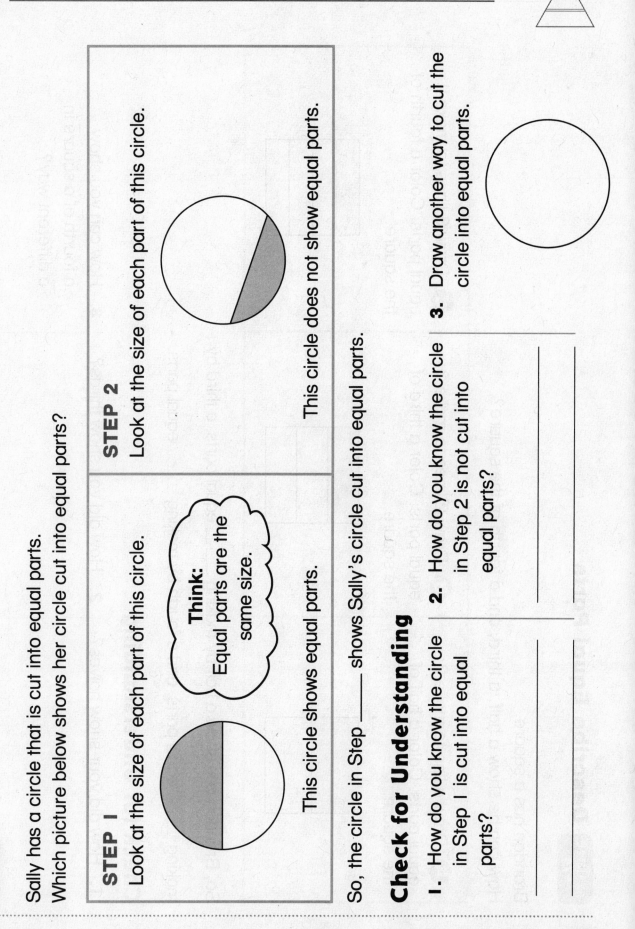

STEP 1

Look at the size of each part of this circle.

Think: Equal parts are the same size.

This circle shows equal parts.

STEP 2

Look at the size of each part of this circle.

This circle does not show equal parts.

So, the circle in Step _____ shows Sally's circle cut into equal parts.

Check for Understanding

1. How do you know the circle in Step 1 is cut into equal parts?

_____

_____

2. How do you know the circle in Step 2 is not cut into equal parts?

_____

_____

3. Draw another way to cut the circle into equal parts.

Extra ball?

Describe Equal Parts

Brandon has a square.
How can he show a half, a third, and a fourth of the square?

A Draw a line to make 2 equal parts. Color a half of the square.

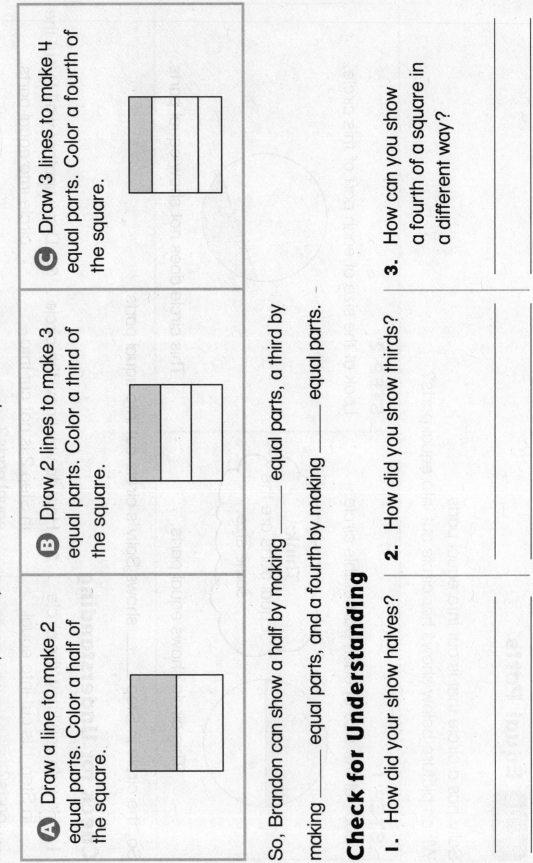

B Draw 2 lines to make 3 equal parts. Color a third of the square.

C Draw 3 lines to make 4 equal parts. Color a fourth of the square.

So, Brandon can show a half by making ____ equal parts, a third by making ____ equal parts, and a fourth by making ____ equal parts.

Check for Understanding

1. How did your show halves?

2. How did you show thirds?

3. How can you show a fourth of a square in a different way?

EXAMPLE E75

Show Equal Parts of a Whole

Abby draws a circle, a rectangle, and square.
How can she make equal parts to show 2 halves, 3 thirds, and 4 fourths?

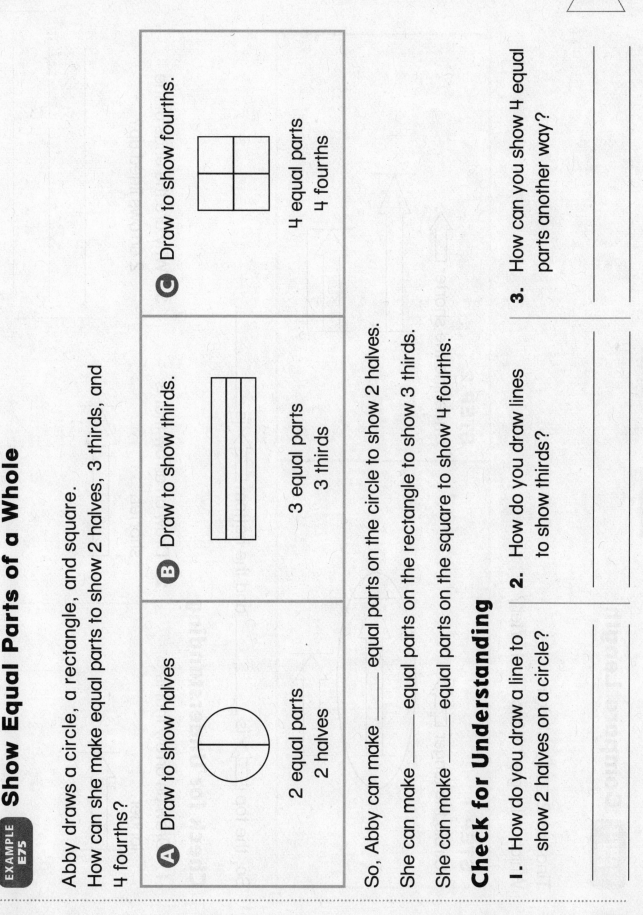

A Draw to show halves

2 equal parts
2 halves

B Draw to show thirds.

3 equal parts
3 thirds

C Draw to show fourths.

4 equal parts
4 fourths

So, Abby can make _____ equal parts on the circle to show 2 halves.

She can make _____ equal parts on the rectangle to show 3 thirds.

She can make _____ equal parts on the square to show 4 fourths.

Check for Understanding

1. How do you draw a line to show 2 halves on a circle?

_____

_____

2. How do you draw lines to show thirds?

_____

_____

3. How can you show 4 equal parts another way?

_____

_____

Compare Length

EXAMPLE E76

Tina has 2 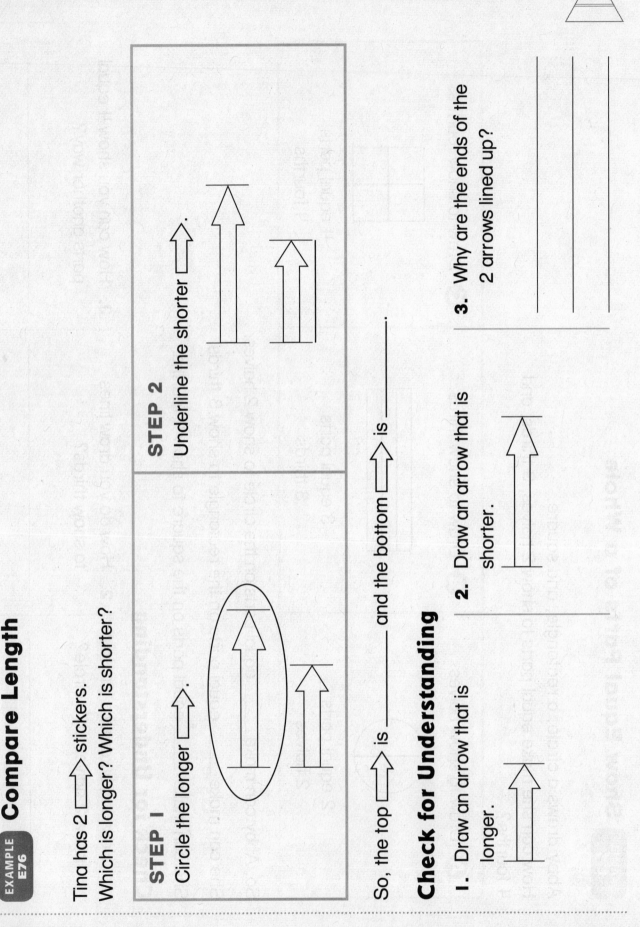 stickers.

Which is longer? Which is shorter?

STEP I

Circle the longer 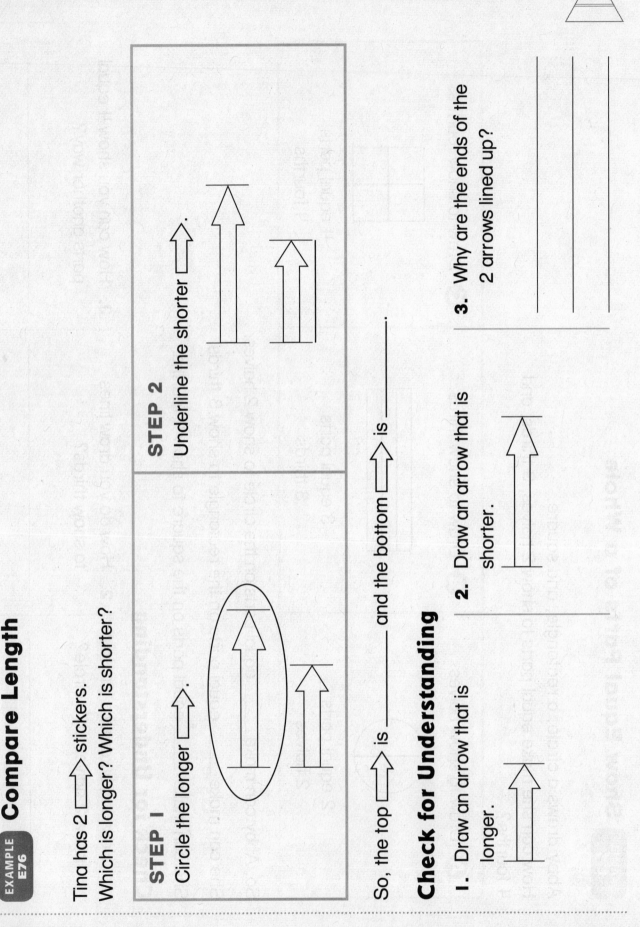.

STEP 2

Underline the shorter 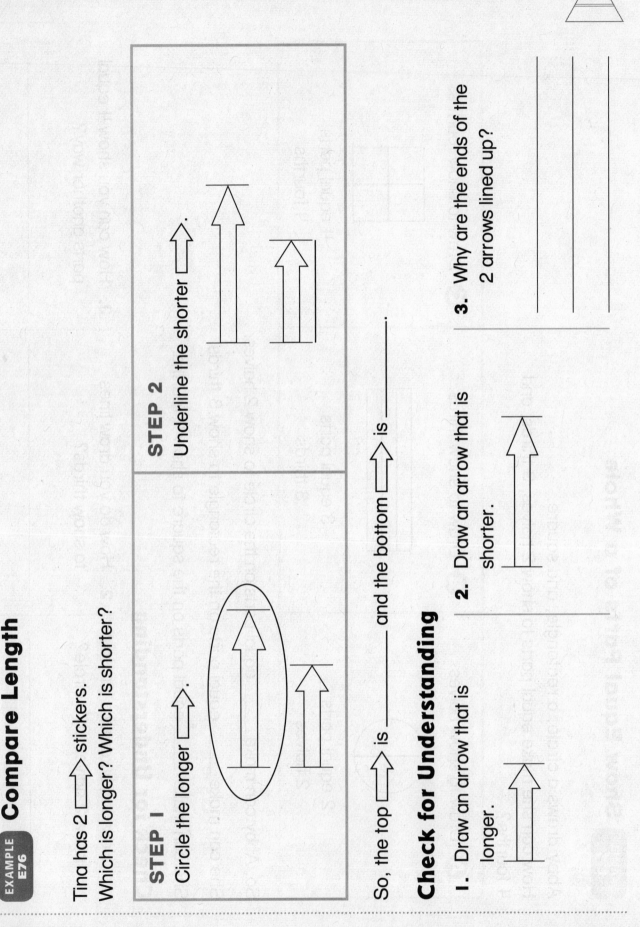.

So, the top 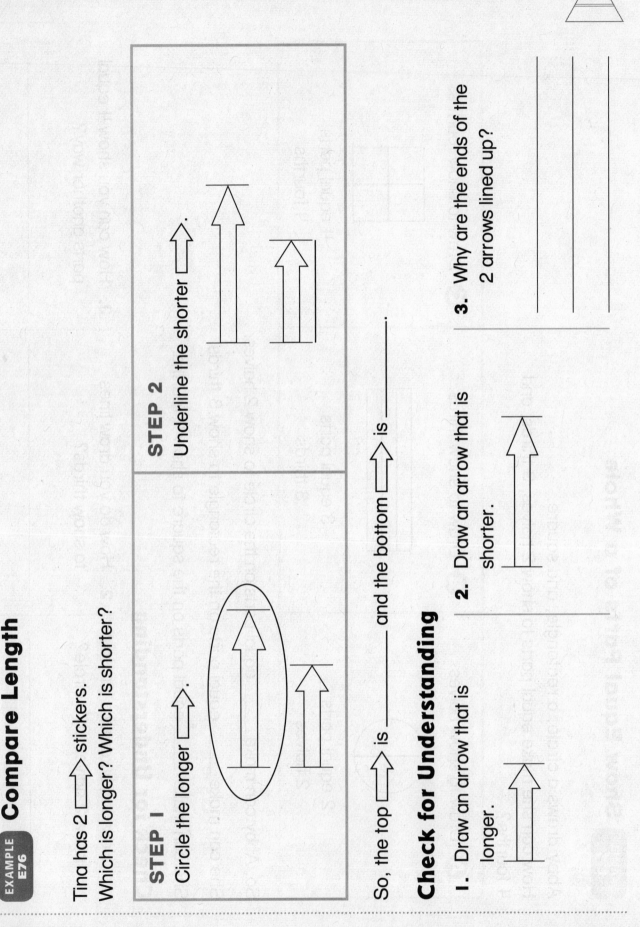 is _____ and the bottom 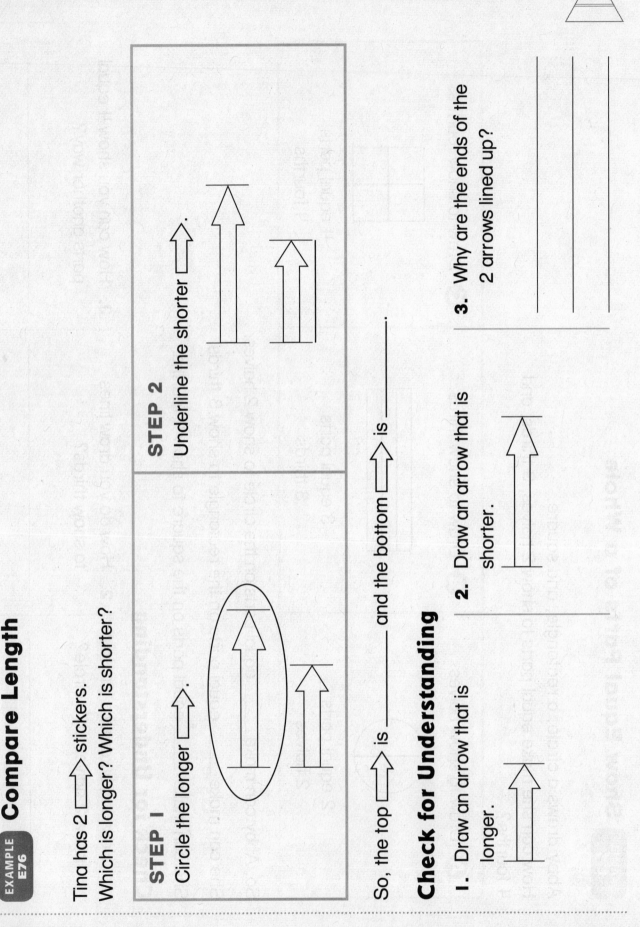 is _____.

Check for Understanding

1. Draw an arrow that is longer.

2. Draw an arrow that is shorter.

3. Why are the ends of the 2 arrows lined up?

_____

_____

_____

EXAMPLE E77 **Order Length**

Max has 2 groups of trucks. Each truck is a different length.
Which group of trucks is in order from shortest to longest?

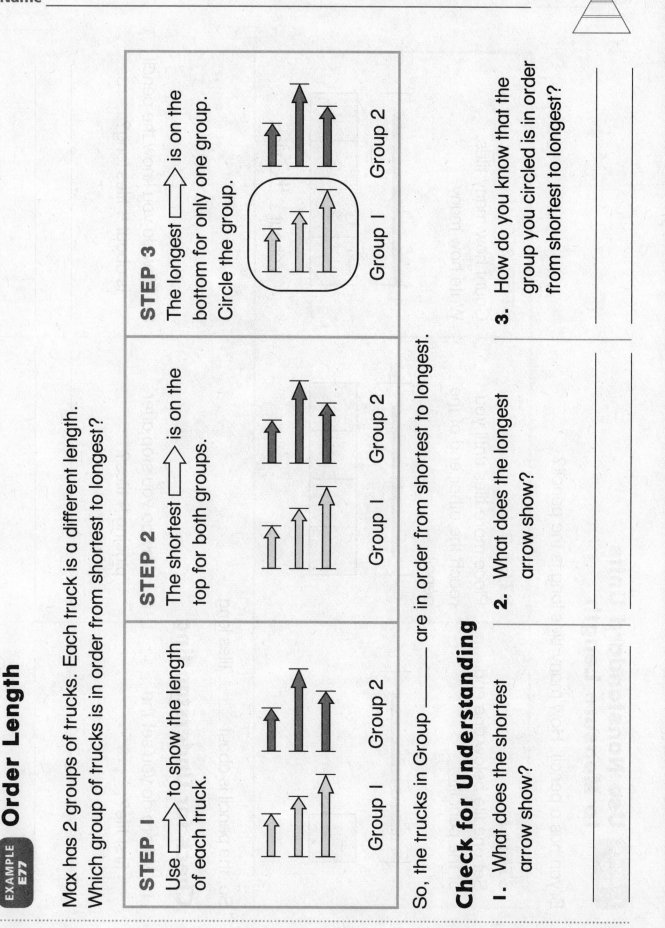

STEP 1

Use ⬆ to show the length of each truck.

Group 1   Group 2

STEP 2

The shortest ⬆ is on the top for both groups.

Group 1   Group 2

STEP 3

The longest ⬆ is on the bottom for only one group. Circle the group.

Group 1   Group 2

So, the trucks in Group _____ are in order from shortest to longest.

Check for Understanding

1. What does the shortest arrow show?

2. What does the longest arrow show?

3. How do you know that the group you circled is in order from shortest to longest?

EXAMPLE E78

Use Nonstandard Units to Measure Length

Bryan has a pencil. How many tiles long is the pencil?

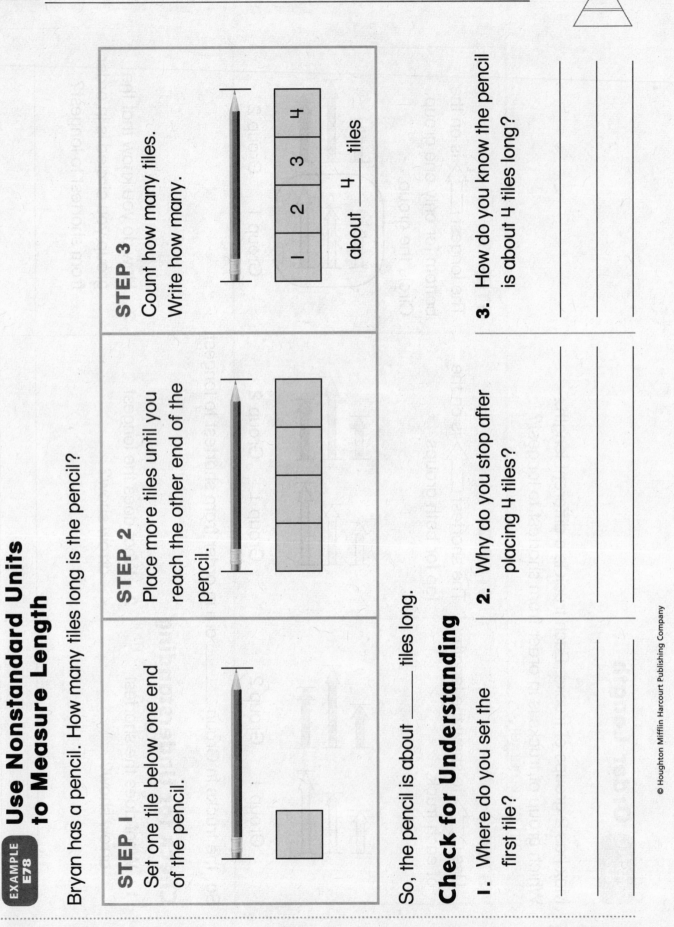

STEP 1

Set one tile below one end of the pencil.

STEP 2

Place more tiles until you reach the other end of the pencil.

STEP 3

Count how many tiles. Write how many.

about ___4___ tiles

So, the pencil is about _____ tiles long.

Check for Understanding

1. Where do you set the first tile?

_____

2. Why do you stop after placing 4 tiles?

_____

3. How do you know the pencil is about 4 tiles long?

_____

_____

_____

EXAMPLE E79

Measure Length Twice: Nonstandard Units

Erin uses 🔗 and 🧊 to measure the length of a marker.

How many 🔗 long is the marker?

How many 🧊 long is the marker?

STEP 1

Measure the length using 🔗 .

about __4__ 🔗

STEP 2

Measure the length using 🧊 .

about __5__ 🧊

So, the marker is about _____ 🔗 long and about _____ 🧊 long.

Check for Understanding

1. How do you know that the marker is about 4 paper clips long?

_____

_____

2. How do you know that the marker is about 5 cubes long?

_____

_____

EXAMPLE E80

Measure with an Inch Ruler

Lori uses a ruler to measure the length of some beads.
What is the length of the beads to the nearest inch?

STEP 1

Line up one end of the beads with 0.

STEP 2

Find the inch mark closest to the other end.

STEP 3

Write the number of inches at that mark.

_4_ inches

So, the beads are ____ inches long.

Check for Understanding

1. How do you line up the beads and the ruler?

_____

_____

2. How do you know which inch mark to find?

_____

_____

3. How do you know the length of the beads is 4 inches?

_____

_____

_____

EXAMPLE E81

Estimate Lengths in Inches

Abby's beads are each 1 inch long.
About how long is Abby's string?

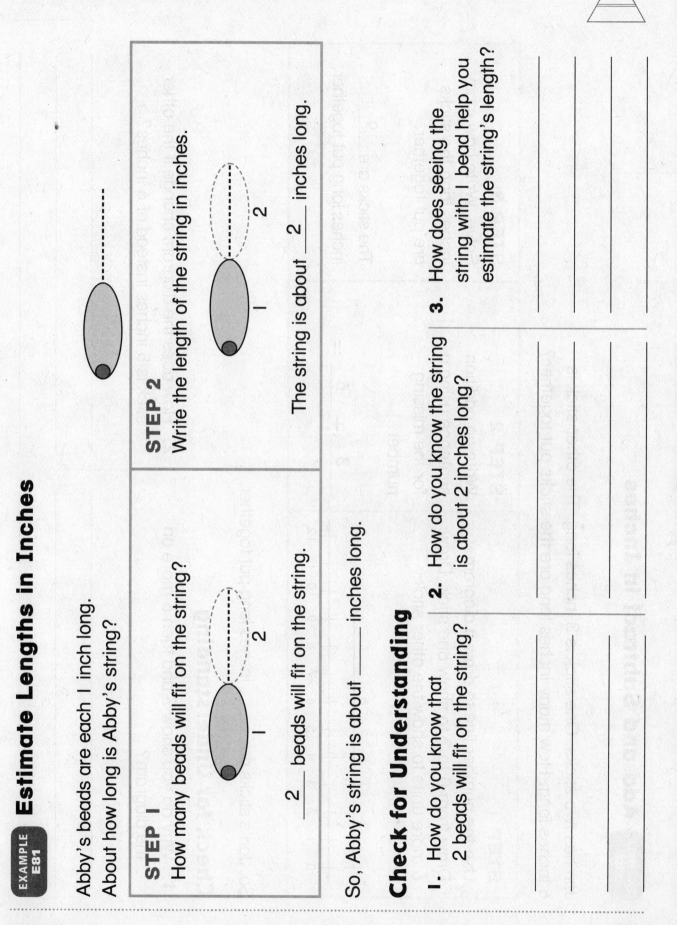

STEP 1

How many beads will fit on the string?

__2__ beads will fit on the string.

STEP 2

Write the length of the string in inches.

The string is about ___ 2 ___ inches long.

So, Abby's string is about _____ inches long.

Check for Understanding

1. How do you know that 2 beads will fit on the string?

2. How do you know the string is about 2 inches long?

3. How does seeing the string with 1 bead help you estimate the string's length?

EXAMPLE E82

Add and Subtract in Inches

Jan has two sticks. One stick is 3 inches long. The other stick is 6 inches long. How many inches long are the sticks put together?

STEP 1

Use the number line to draw a diagram. Draw from 0 to 3 to show one stick. Draw 6 more units to show the other stick.

```
3           6
|---|   |-------|
0 1 2 3 4 5 6 7 8 9 10 11 12
→
```

STEP 2

Write an addition sentence using a ☐ for the missing number.

3 + 6 = ☐

STEP 3

Solve. Write how many inches long the sticks are put together.

The sticks are __9__ inches long put together.

So, Jan's sticks are _____ inches long put together.

Check for Understanding

1. Why do you show 3 and then 6 more on the diagram?

_____

2. How does the diagram change if the other stick is 5 inches instead of 6 inches?

_____

EXAMPLE E83 Measure with a Centimeter Model

Amy has a ribbon. How can Amy use unit cubes to measure the length of the ribbon?

STEP 1

Place unit cubes under the ribbon. Count the unit cubes.

1 2 3 4 5

STEP 2

Write how many unit cubes long the ribbon is.

The ribbon is about __5__ unit cubes long.

STEP 3

Each unit cube is about I centimeter long.

So, the 5 unit cubes are about __5__ centimeters long.

So, the length of the ribbon is about ____ centimeters.

Check for Understanding

1. How do unit cubes help you measure length without a ruler?

_____
_____

2. Why do you know how many unit cubes long the ribbon is?

_____
_____

3. How do you know the length of the ribbon is about 5 centimeters?

_____
_____

Measure with a Centimeter Ruler

Seth has some beads.
What is the length of the beads
to the nearest centimeter?

centimeters

STEP 1

Line up the left end of the
beads with the zero mark
on the ruler.

STEP 2

Find the centimeter mark
closest to the other end of
the bead.

STEP 3

Write the length to the
nearest centimeter.
The beads are about
___4___ centimeters long.

So, the beads are about _____ centimeters long.

Check for Understanding

1. How do you line up the
beads and the ruler?

2. How do you know which
centimeter mark to find?

3. How do you know the
length of the beads is
4 centimeters?

EXAMPLE E85

Centimeters and Meters

Travis wants to measure the length of a bookcase.
What is the length of the bookcase in centimeters?
What is the length of the bookcase in meters?

Think: I meter is the same as 100 centimeters.

STEP 1 Measure the length of the bookcase in centimeters.

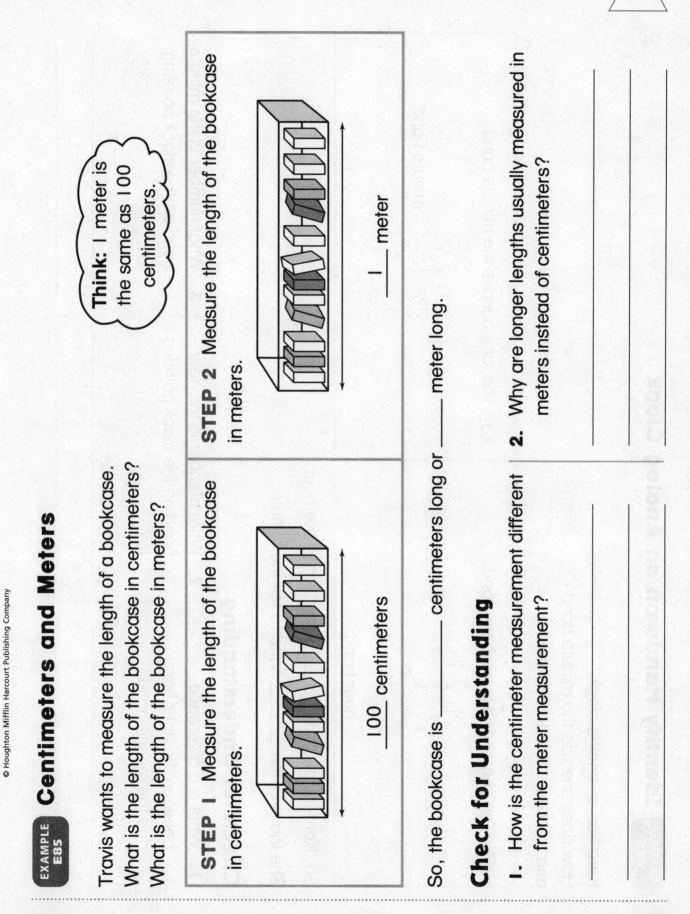

___100___ centimeters

STEP 2 Measure the length of the bookcase in meters.

___I___ meter

So, the bookcase is _____ centimeters long or _____ meter long.

Check for Understanding

1. How is the centimeter measurement different from the meter measurement?

_____

_____

2. Why are longer lengths usually measured in meters instead of centimeters?

_____

_____

EXAMPLE E86   Identify Hands on an Analog Clock

Kara has an analog clock.
How does she use the minute hand
and the hour hand to tell time?

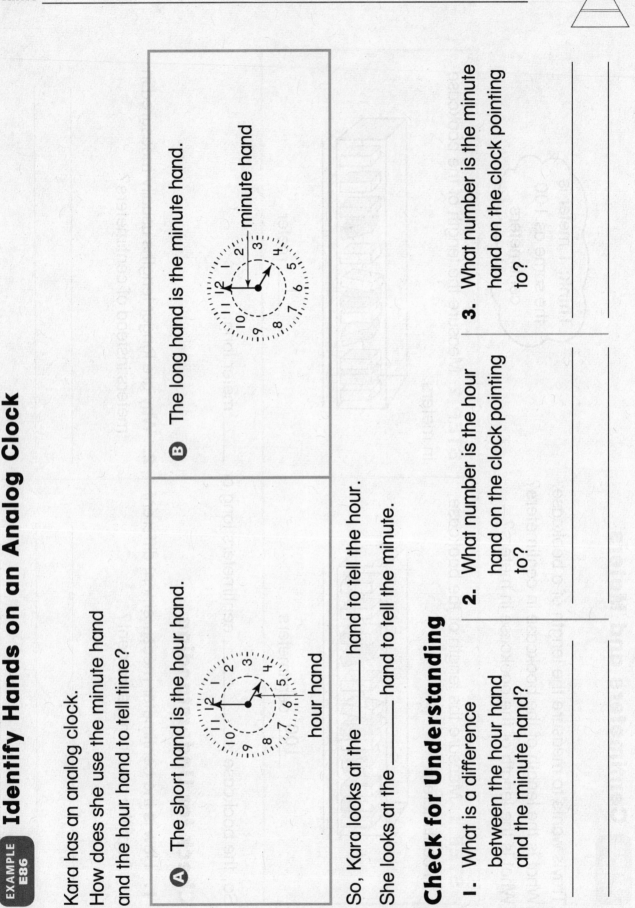

A The short hand is the hour hand.

hour hand

B The long hand is the minute hand.

minute hand

So, Kara looks at the _____ hand to tell the hour.

She looks at the _____ hand to tell the minute.

Check for Understanding

1. What is a difference
   between the hour hand
   and the minute hand?

   _____

   _____

2. What number is the hour
   hand on the clock pointing
   to?

   _____

3. What number is the minute
   hand on the clock pointing
   to?

   _____

Name _____

EXAMPLE E87 **Match Times to the Hour on an Analog and a Digital Clock**

Vic sees an analog clock and a digital clock. Do the clocks show the same time, or do the clocks show different times?

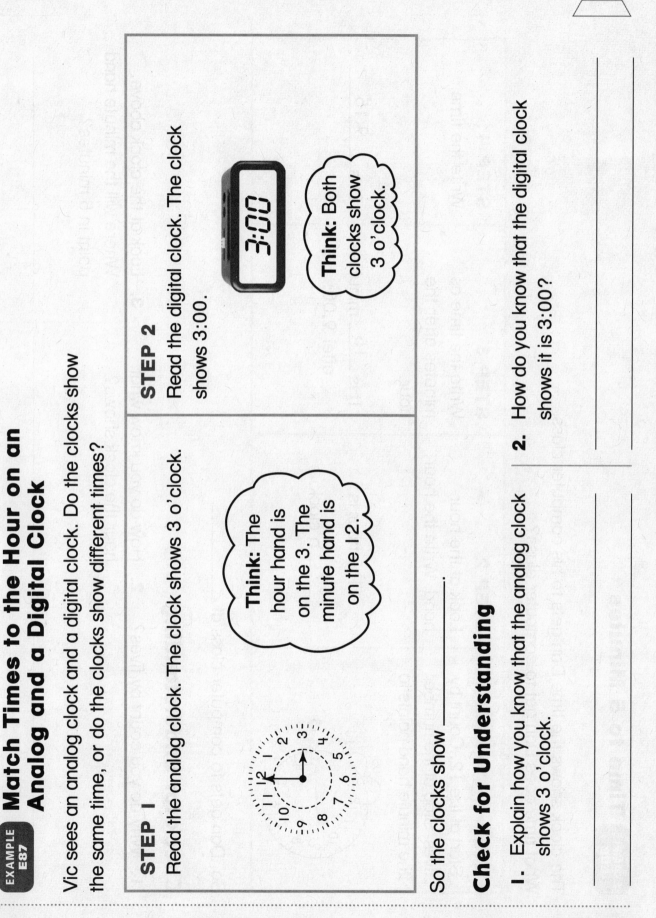

STEP 1

Read the analog clock. The clock shows 3 o'clock.

Think: The hour hand is on the 3. The minute hand is on the 12.

STEP 2

Read the digital clock. The clock shows 3:00.

3:00

Think: Both clocks show 3 o'clock.

So the clocks show _____ .

Check for Understanding

1. Explain how you know that the analog clock shows 3 o'clock.

2. How do you know that the digital clock shows it is 3:00?

EXAMPLE E88 Time to 5 Minutes

The clock shows the time Dan gets to his computer class.
What time does Dan get to computer class?

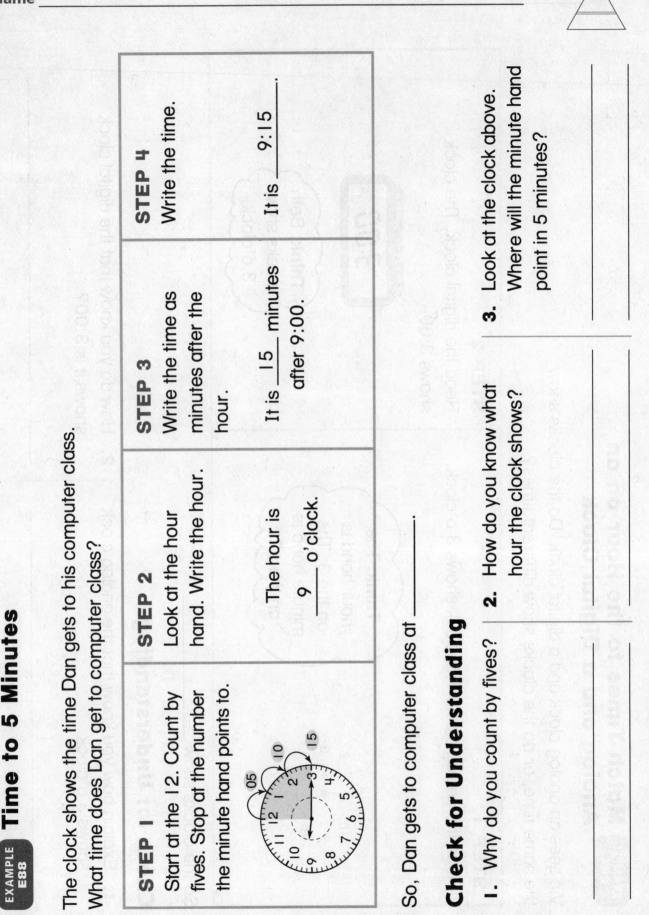

STEP 1

Start at the 12. Count by fives. Stop at the number the minute hand points to.

STEP 2

Look at the hour hand. Write the hour.

The hour is

9 o'clock.

STEP 3

Write the time as minutes after the hour.

It is _15_ minutes after 9:00.

STEP 4

Write the time.

It is __9:15__ .

So, Dan gets to computer class at _____ .

Check for Understanding

1. Why do you count by fives?

2. How do you know what hour the clock shows?

3. Look at the clock above. Where will the minute hand point in 5 minutes?

EXAMPLE E89

Pennies and Dimes

Tony has 4 🪙 in his pocket.
How many cents does he have?

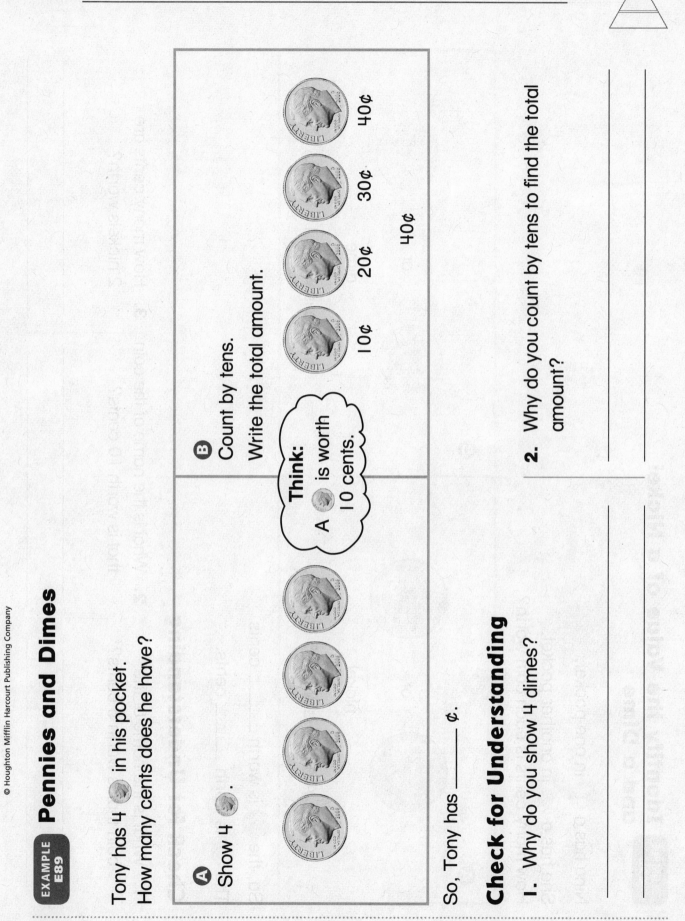

A Show 4 🪙 .

Think:

A 🪙 is worth 10 cents.

B Count by tens.
Write the total amount.

10¢   20¢   30¢   40¢

40¢

So, Tony has _____ ¢.

Check for Understanding

1. Why do you show 4 dimes?

2. Why do you count by tens to find the total amount?

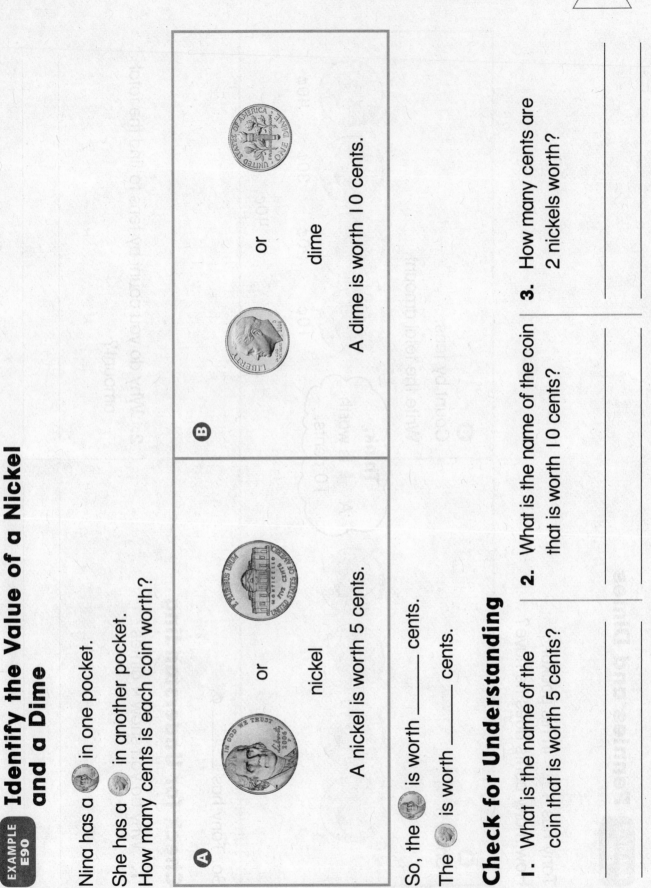

Identify the Value of a Nickel and a Dime

Nina has a 🪙 in one pocket.

She has a 🪙 in another pocket.

How many cents is each coin worth?

A

or

nickel

A nickel is worth 5 cents.

B

or

dime

A dime is worth 10 cents.

So, the 🪙 is worth _____ cents.

The 🪙 is worth _____ cents.

Check for Understanding

1. What is the name of the coin that is worth 5 cents?

2. What is the name of the coin that is worth 10 cents?

3. How many cents are 2 nickels worth?

© Houghton Mifflin Harcourt Publishing Company

EXAMPLE E91 **One Dollar**

Tanya has 10 dimes. How much money does Tanya have?

STEP 1 Count on by tens.

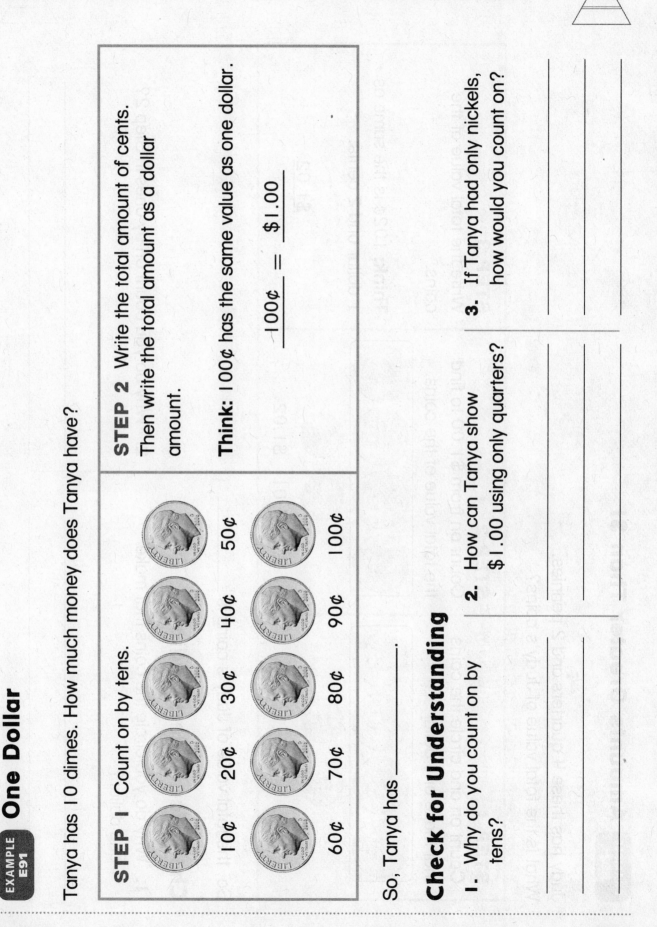

10¢ 20¢ 30¢ 40¢ 50¢

60¢ 70¢ 80¢ 90¢ 100¢

STEP 2 Write the total amount of cents.

Then write the total amount as a dollar amount.

Think: 100¢ has the same value as one dollar.

$$100¢ = \$1.00$$

So, Tanya has _____.

Check for Understanding

1. Why do you count on by tens?

2. How can Tanya show $1.00 using only quarters?

3. If Tanya had only nickels, how would you count on?

Amounts Greater Than $1

EXAMPLE E92

Judy has these 4 quarters and 2 pennies.
What is the total value of Judy's coins?

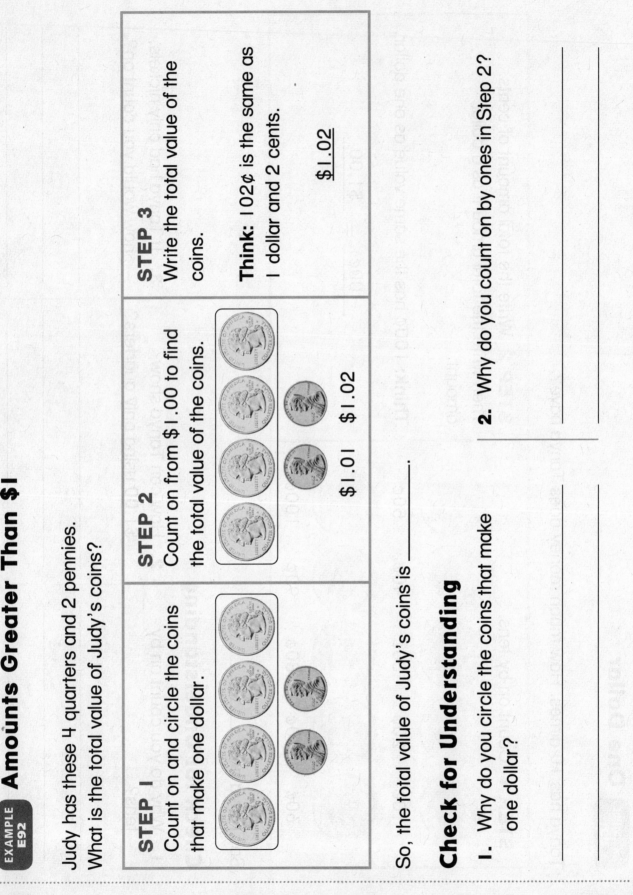

STEP 1

Count on and circle the coins that make one dollar.

STEP 2

Count on from $1.00 to find the total value of the coins.

$1.01 $1.02

STEP 3

Write the total value of the coins.

Think: 102¢ is the same as 1 dollar and 2 cents.

$1.02

So, the total value of Judy's coins is _____ .

Check for Understanding

1. Why do you circle the coins that make one dollar?

_____

_____

2. Why do you count on by ones in Step 2?

_____

_____

EXAMPLE E93

Read Picture Graphs

Abby makes a picture graph to show some children's favorite shapes.

Use Abby's picture graph.
Which shape did more children choose?

Favorite Shapes

squares	⚎	⚎	
● circles	⚎	⚎	⚎

Each ⚎ stands for 1 child.

STEP 1

Write how many children each figure stands for.

⚎ = ___1___ child

STEP 2

Write how many children chose each shape.

__2__ children chose squares.

__3__ children chose circles.

STEP 3

Circle the sentence that tells which shape more children chose.

2 children chose squares.

(3 children chose circles.)

So, more children chose _____.

Check for Understanding

1. How do you know that 2 children chose squares?

2. How do you know that more children chose circles than squares?

EXAMPLE E94

Make Tally Charts

Ann has these star and flower stickers.

Does Ann have more star or flower stickers?

Make a tally chart to solve.

STEP 1

Make a row in the tally chart for stars. Draw a tally for each star. Write the total number of stars.

Stickers		Total
stars	IIII	4

STEP 2

Make a row in the tally chart for flowers. Draw a tally for each flower. Write the total number of flowers.

Stickers		Total
stars	IIII	4
flowers	IIII II	7

STEP 3

Compare the total number of stars and flowers.

There are 4 stars.

There are 7 flowers.

7 is greater than 4.

So, Ann has more _____ stickers.

Check for Understanding

1. What does each tally mark stand for?

_____

_____

2. Why do you cross 4 tallies in the row for flowers?

_____

_____

3. How do you know Ann has more flower stickers?

_____

_____

EXAMPLE E95

Read Bar Graphs

The bar graph shows how many of each color cube Rob has. How many blue cubes does Rob have?

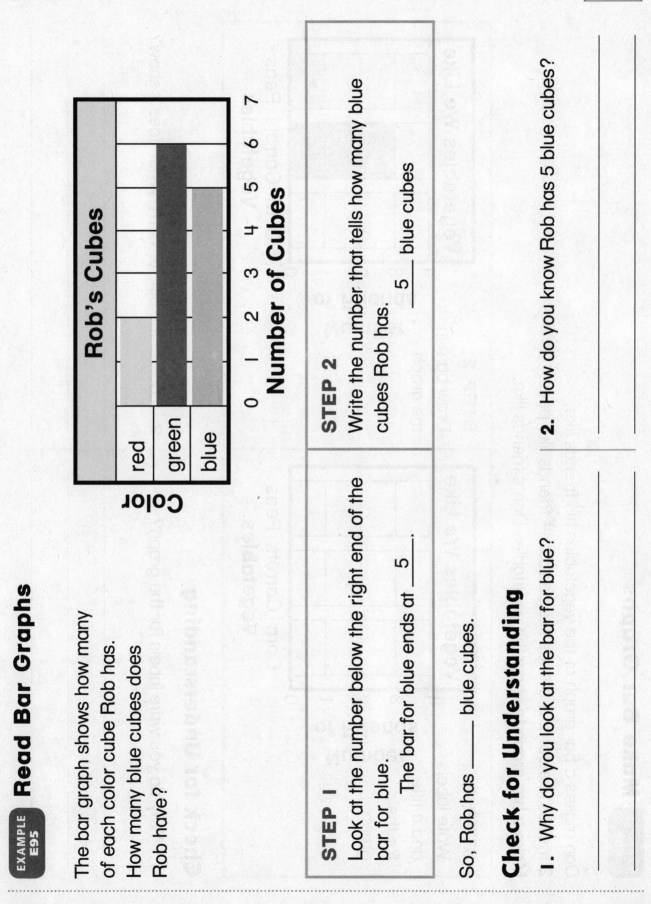

Rob's Cubes

STEP 1

Look at the number below the right end of the bar for blue.

The bar for blue ends at ___5___.

So, Rob has ___ blue cubes.

STEP 2

Write the number that tells how many blue cubes Rob has.

___5___ blue cubes

Check for Understanding

1. Why do you look at the bar for blue?

_____

_____

2. How do you know Rob has 5 blue cubes?

_____

_____

Make Bar Graphs

EXAMPLE E96

Dan makes a bar graph of the vegetables his friends like.
2 friends like corn. 3 friends like carrots. 4 friends like peas.
Make a bar graph to show the vegetables Dan's friends like.

STEP 1
Write labels
and a title
for the
graph.

STEP 2
Draw bars in
the graph.

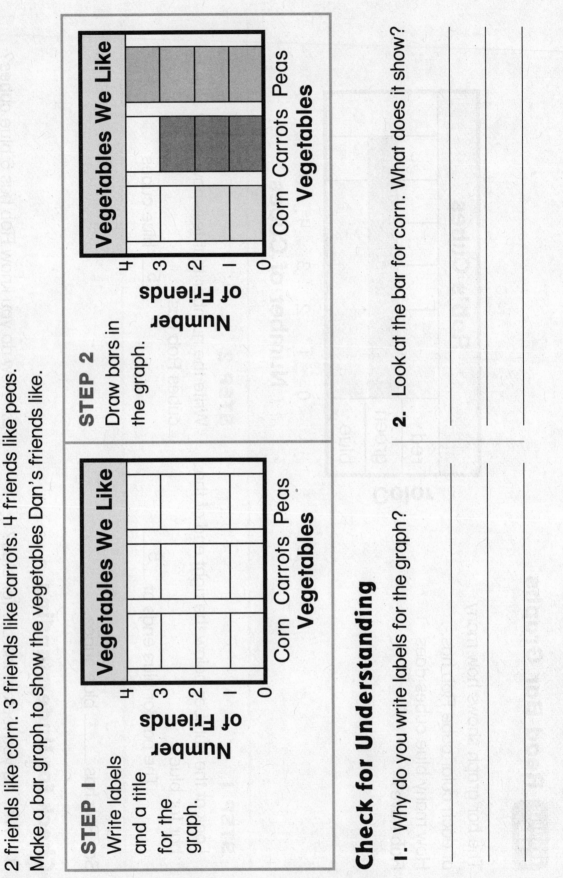

Check for Understanding

1. Why do you write labels for the graph? _____

2. Look at the bar for corn. What does it show? _____